T0282851

On Murder:

"For a man to commit mu

"The best way to kill a man is not to confide in anybody. keep it just between yourself—you can't trust everybody."

"The next best thing to do in killing a man is to leave a gun on his person, which is a good case, because the Police Department of the City of New York says: 'What the hell, that's another one gone,' and the case is forgotten about. They don't interest themselves too much in the case where gangsters are killed."

On Police:

"Treat 'em nice . . . Then, if I get into trouble you may be able to do business with 'em."

"I wouldn't squeal on any cop, which ain't in me to be a rat. Squealing on anybody is being a rat."

On Politicians:

"In order to make a buck, you got to give a buck. What I mean, if you are going to make it, you got to spend it. So you go and make yourself connection with the leader of your district. Well, as you know, everything is political all over the country. Every district carries a captain. Probably you do a lot of work for that captain on election."

On Stealing Elections:

"You steal the votes and tear them up. The party that is in has always got the power of that city. . . . You can vote ten times yourself without being recognized, because if a party does not show up to vote on election day you vote for him anyway, and if there is anybody there on the opposite side, like a poll watcher, he is afraid that he will get hurt, and keeps his mouth shut."

"We honestly believe that the author, Danny Ahearn, could commit any crime and get away with it."

—*Wilmington News-Journal*

"I cannot see any good purpose or any social benefit to be derived from such a book. This might be otherwise but for the very exactness with which the author lays down the best and most certain rules for committing a murder, for robbing a jewelry store, for stealing an automobile . . . for the commission of every crime on the calendar 'and getting away with it.'"

—*Nashville Banner*

"a truly dangerous book"

—*Lansing State Journal*

"a thoroughly vicious book"

—*Monrovia News-Post*

"So genuine is the picture and so is the criminal psychology revealed that it is difficult for the uninitiated to realize that there is in our midst a group of people who think differently, live differently, and react differently to all social standards and customs."

—*Wichita Falls Times*

"Danny Ahearn tells everything but one essential—how to acquire the nerve to kill a man and how to get rid of a guilty conscience after it is done."

—*Victoria Daily Times*

"Even salacious or sexy trash is less harmful . . . One hopes to read some day soon that the person responsible for letting [this] volume get into the hands of the two Winnipeg boys has been apprehended and fittingly punished. He is more responsible for the eight burglaries said to have been committed by the boys than are the lads themselves."

—*Edmonton Journal*

Acknowledgments

The staff of Staccato Crime would like to thank Katrina Aliashkevich and Zoë Vorzimmer for research assistance, and Gary Lovisi would like to give special thanks to Lucille Cali.

HOW TO COMMIT
A MURDER
by
DANNY AHEARN

Introduction by
Gary Lovisi

AN IMPRINT OF STARK HOUSE PRESS

HOW TO COMMIT A MURDER
Copyright ©1930 by Ives Washburn

Published by Staccato Crime
An imprint of Stark House Press
1315 H Street
Eureka, CA 95501, USA
griffinskye3@sbcglobal.net
www.starkhousepress.com

"Oh Danny Boy!" ©2022 by Gary Lovisi

ISBN: 978-1-951473-90-7
Staccato Crime: SC-006

All Staccato Crime titles are edited and produced
by David Rachels and Jeff Vorzimmer.
Book series design by *¡caliente!Design*, Austin, Texas

This is a work of fiction. Names, characters, places and incidents are either the
products of the author's imagination or used fictionally, and any resemblance to
actual persons, living or dead, events or locales, is entirely coincidental.

First Staccato Crime Edition: July 2022

Preface

When our friend Gary Lovisi brought a copy of *How to Commit a Murder* to us for consideration as a perfect title for the Staccato Crime imprint, I devoured the book. I agreed wholeheartedly.

What I found most compelling about the book was the fact that it was written entirely in the criminal vernacular of the Twenties. Fortunately for the modern reader of this wonderful book, the editors at Ives Washburn, to whom the book was brought—actually, the *idea* of the book—maintained Ahearn's unique voice throughout the editing process and by doing so, created a minor masterpiece of crime literature.

Another thing that struck me was Ahearn's use of "good fellows" as synonymous with "wiseguys." In fact the word "wiseguy" doesn't appear anywhere in *How to Commit a Murder,* as its use to mean a "made man" in the Mob, and hence someone you could trust, wouldn't come into vogue for decades. "Good fellow(s)" however appears some twenty times, not specifically in reference to someone "connected" with the Mob, but someone in the underworld who could be trusted.

It would be another sixty years before the connection was made for the general public when Nicholas Pileggi's book *Wiseguy*, about gangster Henry Hill, became Martin Scorsese's film *Goodfellas*. Early in the film Hill explains, "You know, we always called each other goodfellas. Like you'd say to somebody: 'You're gonna like this guy, he's all right. He's a goodfella. He's one of us.' You understand? We were goodfellas, wiseguys."

You're gonna like this guy, Danny Ahearn. He's a goodfella.

Jeff Vorzimmer
Austin, Texas
The Ides of March, 2022

Oh, Danny Boy!

You are about to embark upon one of the most extraordinary reading experiences you have ever encountered in crime writing, so prepare yourself to meet Danny Ahearn!

Danny Ahearn was born Daniel Francis A'Hearn on September 8, 1901, the oldest of nine children. Not much is known about his early life aside from his writings and various newspaper clippings. We do know from newspaper reports that in 1926 he was wounded in a gun battle in Brooklyn where two men were killed, was allegedly shot by Bugsy Siegel in 1928, and barely survived an attempt on his life in Cleveland in 1929.

He married Sarah Davis on November 18, 1932. In 1934 he received 2½ years in New York's notorious Sing Sing Prison for fraud. His second term there, also for fraud, came in 1937. The last we hear of Danny is in a 1948 clipping where it states that at 45 years of age, he was sentenced to 20 years to life for robbery. The judge said he gave him that long a sentence because he was a fourth-time offender. "Dapper Daniel Francis Ahearn," as he was called, was angry at the judge for that tough verdict and shouted defiantly at him, "I thought Hitler was dead!" He should have stuck to the writing game—he coulda been a contender—but the lure of criminality proved too strong. Danny died in Manhattan on November 3, 1960.

Prior to the 1930 publication of *How to Commit a Murder*, Danny Ahearn was not a writer of any sort. Later on he would work as a reporter for *The Daily Worker* and several newspapers, as well as a scriptwriter for Warner Brothers in Hollywood in 1932-33. In 1930, however, Danny was a career criminal, and this book is a manual of sorts for the aspiring career criminal. Danny talks about every manner of crime—all of which he had proudly committed, or had intimate knowledge of—and he tells his story in the rough, politically incorrect jargon of the hot and heavy era of The Roaring Twenties.

How to Commit a Murder takes you down deep and dirty into Danny's criminal mind, and it is a truly frightening place!

Chapters include such charming titles as "How to Rob a Jewelry Store"; "How to Stickup a Fur Joint"; "Beating a Frameup"; "How to Commit a Murder—"; and "—And Get Away with It."

I think by now you get the point. It is a fascinating and chilling story by a young man (just 28 years of age when it was written) who was both charming and intelligent. This makes for a devastating combination.

Before we get to Danny's story, we are treated to a most interesting introduction of how the book came about by John S. Clapp ("J.S.C."), who was in charge of acquisitions, sales, and promotion at the publisher, Ives Washburn, from 1930 to 1932. Meanwhile, the only name actually mentioned in the book— Danny certainly does not mention any of his "associates" by name—as he says, "he ain't no rat"—is someone named George Bye.

So who is George Bye? Bye (1887–1957) was a prominent literary agent prior to World War II who rose to fame on so-called "stunt" books—books by people who were popular in the news. He was the literary agent for Eleanor Roosevelt, Charles Lindbergh, Alexander Woollcott, and others. He was a key mover and shaker in the publishing scene. He knew Danny Ahearn "through a friend" and was also a friend of John S. Clapp. Bye told Clapp, "I don't want to make a penny on him [Ahearn] . . . Count me out. Everything he makes on the book is his."

When told this, Danny replied about Bye, "He's a swell guy."

It appears that both Bye and Clapp knew not only that Danny Ahearn had a chilling story to tell in this book but that he was the genuine article, so they wanted to keep their distance from him. I believe they thought Danny might have been a bit . . . dangerous.

Nevertheless, Danny Ahearn was the perfect man to write such a book. At the time he had been tried 22 times for various crimes, and convicted only twice! Of his two murder charges, both were thrown out! For lack of evidence. It appears he did get away with murder! When Danny was asked by Clapp about his qualifications to write a book for them on crime, he proudly produced a resume in the form of an envelope full of newspaper clippings denoting his long array of crimes. Well, as they say, "Nuff said," and Clapp was sold.

Three years after the publication of *How to Commit a Murder,* Hollywood came calling with at least three Pre-Code films being based on Danny's stories. This was an era when gangsters like Bonnie & Clyde and John Dillinger were robbing banks at will, were considered heroes by some in the public, and were often shown with sympathy in gangster films. Danny's first film, *Wild Boys of the Road* (1933), directed by William A. Wellman, was based on his story "Desperate Youth." That same year, *Picture Snatcher* appeared with James Cagney in an early role playing the part of "Danny," an ex-con newspaper photographer, based on Ahearn's story of the same title. *Picture Snatcher* would be remade in 1942 under the title *Escape from Crime*, introducing a very young Jackie Gleason. In 1936, *Bulldog Edition* appeared, based on Danny's newspaperman story "Back in Circulation." Ahearn, who now considered himself to be a writer, also produced at least one novel, *Charity Girl* (Macaulay & Co., 1936), about a "philandering philanthropist."

In 1930, *How to Commit a Murder* appeared in a UK edition, published by George Routledge under the less sensational title *Confessions of a Gunman.* In his preface to this edition, famed writer, poet, and critic Richard Church (1893–1972) offers a judgmental look at Danny and his book. He writes, "I am anxious to introduce it because I feel myself under an obligation to warn the reader that it will probably be one of the most horrible books he has ever experienced." He goes on in this vein for many pages. In fact, Church is so appalled by Danny's criminal mind and atrocious activities, it is as if he has encountered a creature alien to humanity. He sees one redeeming aspect of the book, and that is its value to sociologists and other professionals in their studies of this type of human monster. In some ways Church was correct, but I believe that Danny was less complicated than all that. Danny might have said that he was just a regular guy out to look for opportunities to make a fast buck—*any way that he could!*

The casual manner and calm banality of Danny's criminous narration is surely chilling. All that said, what makes this new Staccato Crime edition so special? It is Danny Ahearn himself, telling his own unique story in his own words—raw and uncensored! This new edition is really something special and long overdue. Prepare yourself for an incredible ride!

> *Oh, Danny Boy!*
> *The pipes, the pipes, are calling!*

Gary Lovisi
Brooklyn, New York
St. Valentine's Day, 2022

GARY LOVISI is the editor of the classic crime magazine *Hardboiled*, as well as *Paperback Parade*. He is the author of the ultra-hardboiled Vic Powers and Griff & Fats series, and is an MWA Edgar Award-nominated author. He has contributed introductions for various Stark House editions and is the author of the books *Sherlock Holmes & Mr. Mac* (Black Gat Book #11) and *A Sherlock Holmes Notebook* (Stark House). You can find out more about him and his work at his website, www.gryphonbooks.com; his Facebook page; and through his *YouTube* channel videos.

Cover of the First Edition, 1930

Several months ago the publishers went to George Bye, a well-known literary agent, to ask him if he could find someone to write a book on the third degree for them. They felt that if he liked the idea he would find the one man to do it. The present writer, more or less responsible for the suggestion in the first place, was given the handling of the matter.

Mr. Bye proved enthusiastic, and I could almost see the book between covers. But to find the ideal person didn't prove so easy. After several meetings we decided to drop the matter for the time being.

One day, about three weeks later, Bye called me on the phone.

"I've got just the man for you!" he exclaimed without any preliminaries. "I'm sending him right over."

A few moments later Mr. Ahearn was announced.

"I'm Danny Ahearn," he stated, pumping my hand a bit too confidentially. My heart sank. I had expected a newspaper man with plenty of police and court experience who would do the book in good journalese and would have the necessary experience and acumen to dig out facts.

"Sport writer—tabloid," I thought.

"I am very glad to know you, Mr. Ahearn," I said. "Come on inside."

We lighted cigarettes. There was an uneasy silence for a moment. Then the telephone rang. It was Mr. Bye.

"Is Ahearn there? Fine! You know I'm not his agent. No. Met him through a friend of mine. Now, I like him a lot. I don't want to make a penny on him. So you make your own arrangements. Anything you say is O.K. Sure, he knows the stuff cold. Yes, that's right. Count me out. Everything he makes on the book is his."

"That was Mr. Bye," I said.

"O.K.," said Danny.

"He says, that he would rather have you deal direct with us; he wants no commission."

"He's a swell guy."

"Do you know about the book we had in mind?" I asked, approaching the subject gently. I was becoming more and more convinced that there was something not quite right. Danny took a deep drag on his cigarette.

"Yes, I know all about it," he said, almost as if from memory. "I can do a good book for you. And I want to do it." That evidently decided the matter. All that was left was to sign a contract. But I wasn't convinced.

"Are you sure you know what we want?"

"Yes. A book about the third degree, ain't it? I know all about the third degree. I can do a good book for you. And I want to write it."

"What are your credentials, Mr. Ahearn?" I was still unconvinced. "What have you written before that would qualify you for this job?"

Danny reached into his pocket and pulled out a tattered envelope which he handed to me without comment. Inside were fifteen or twenty newspaper clippings in all hues under the sun and from every part of the country. I chose a pink one. It was a three-column spread, two-column article, and the heading ran as follows:

DANNY AHEARN SHOT IN CLEVELAND!
DYING IN HOSPITAL WITH FOUR
BULLETS IN STOMACH!

Now I pride myself on playing an average game of poker. But evidently I couldn't keep my astonishment out of my face, for Danny smiled and watched me shrewdly as I perused the details of his career. Together with an account of the shooting there was a complete biographical sketch of the principal character taken from the newspaper's "morgue," or file material concerning persons of probable news value. From it I learnt that Danny was twenty-eight years old, had been booked in New York on major charges twenty-two times, and had (as he himself would say) "beaten the rap" twenty times. He had served terms in Elmira and Sing Sing. He had been tried twice on the charge of murder, and twice acquitted for lack of evidence. He had been charged at one time or another with all the major crimes, and he held all records for "beating the rap." Prominent in underworld circles from coast to coast, he had connections in all the large cities of the country. And much more. I read on with increasing astonishment, then looked up. Danny smiled again.

"That's a record," he said modestly.

"It sure is," I agreed, a bit weakly. "You've had a most interesting life. And I can see you have a book of some kind in you. But how does all this qualify you to write about the third degree?"

Danny became serious.

"Listen, mister! I have been given the third degree by every big city in the country. Who's better qualified?"

Still I hedged.

"You might be prejudiced," I ventured. "We want a man who has not been in the racket himself, who will be impartial, and whom people will believe."

Then Danny talked. He began by describing third degree methods in New York, then jumped to Detroit and Chicago, Pittsburgh and Buffalo.

"In Cleveland," said Danny finally, "they had a special trick. The inspector would make you stand in front of him. He'd lean back in his chair and cross his legs. Then he would ask questions. If you answered the way you were supposed to answer, O.K. If you didn't the inspector would shoot out with his foot (Danny gave a very convincing demonstration), kick you in the stomach and throw you to the other side of the room. So," he continued, "after being questioned in this manner for several hours, when I was brought before the judge the next morning I couldn't stand up straight, my stomach was so sore.

"'Why don't you stand up straight when you're addressing the court, Mr. Ahearn?' the judge asked.

"'I can't, your honor,' I tells him.

"'Why not?' says the judge. 'I fell downstairs your honor,' I tells him."

"For God's sake!" I exclaimed in amazement. "Why didn't you show those cops up? Why didn't you tell the judge what happened? You had your proof. Why did you let the cops get away with it?"

Danny looked highly shocked.

"What! Squeal on the cops? They wouldn't trust me no more! I gotta do business with those guys!"

Here indeed was a point of view! This man was the real thing. I decided the time had come to plunge.

I realized that I must not be too personal. But ever since our conversation began those two trials on a capital charge with the tantalizing words "acquitted for lack of evidence," had haunted my mind. I framed my question carefully.

"What sort of third degree do they give you for murder?"

The answer was prompt and unexpected.

"They don't give you no third degree for murder."

"Why ever not?"

"Because you get it all fixed before you give yourself up."

"Give yourself up? for murder?"

"Sure."

"Don't you get caught?"

"Only amateurs get caught."

"Oh! But"—I hesitated—"what's the advantage in giving yourself up?"

"So's you can get tried and discharged. So's you won't have it hanging over you for the rest of your life! See?"

I saw. It was the double jeopardy provision in the Constitution. No man can be put in jeopardy of his life twice for the same offense.

"But how do you get it fixed up?" I continued.

"Listen, mister," said Danny, and began. He told me how one went about covering one's tracks after committing a murder, then branched out into a description of the underworld and its professions. All unconsciously he gave me the underworld's point of view, which is his own—the underworld's code of ethics, its needs, and its safeguards against attack. He made me realize for the first time that there existed in our midst a people as foreign to our own society as any group of raw immigrants—a group that thought differently, lived differently, and reacted differently to social standards and customs. Prompted occasionally by a question he talked for four and a half solid hours—from two-thirty to seven—painting a picture of the underworld which was fascinating in its color and intimacy.

"Will you put all that into a book?" I asked finally.

"Sure I will. Anything you say. And not a thing I can't prove."

And that is the way *How to Commit a Murder* was conceived. The actual writing presented a problem. If there had been a dictagraph installed in the office we might almost have had Danny's book ready for the printer that afternoon, so clear, straight, and to the point his story had been. But there was no dictagraph, and it was obvious that for Ahearn to write the book was out of the question. Danny himself knew it.

"I'm not a writer," he explained, "I'm a gambler. I'll tell it to someone who understands books. Let him write it. That's his business."

But an ordinary "ghost" would scarcely do. He would lose the flavor of Ahearn's speech, and might slip ideas of his own into the text. Eventually it was decided to let Ahearn talk in the presence of an expert stenographer, who would take down everything that was said.

Ahearn spent every evening for the better part of three weeks with the present writer, retelling his story. The following pages are the result.

This book concerns itself primarily with how the underworld makes its living. It should be noted that a social structure so organized as to permit its individual members to accumulate unequal portions of the world's goods is a society which must support this underworld. The desire for wealth leads to all crimes except those of passion. If robbery were safe, or only slightly punishable, then robbers would be our only professional criminals. We would have no "business" murders, no dope selling, no hijacking. Gangsters are thieves made desperate by the difficulty of thieving. Then murder enters the field. Protect a thief and prevent a murder—this is sound underworld doctrine, part of a rigid code of ethics, rigidly enforced wherever crook meets crook. To break down this code we have a third degree system. We have also that individual, so thoroughly despised in the underworld and police circles—the rat, more commonly known as stool-pigeon. The rat goes against the code. The gunman goes against the rat. And in his active support is enlisted all the complicated society of the underworld. For the gunman is its supreme ruler as well as its policeman, who keeps order in this tremendous disorder. He interprets justice and metes out punishment. He is the outstanding paradox of a world of social paradox.

This phenomenon is explained in the following chapters. When Danny tells us how to stick up a fur joint he not only describes preparations, precautions, and alibis of the mob; he shows us their reactions to cops, their ideas concerning honesty and loyalty and profits, their attitude toward the people robbed. "Treat 'em nice," says Danny. "Then, if I get into trouble you may be able to do business with 'em." For that reason the "wise guy" uses handcuffs instead of rope to secure his victims—surgeon's plaster "because it comes off easy" instead of rags for gags. The only thing he uses plenty of and with violence—is talk. Talk is cheap and can always be apologized for.

Very few names are mentioned in the book. A good thief doesn't rat. A man's private life, even after death, is sacred. Two men may hate each other—that's in the code. They will seek each other out by fair means and foul; but neither will give the other away. But they know they must be loyal to each other against their common enemy if they are to exist at all. Before he signed the contract for his book Ahearn stipulated that he was to mention no names and to give away no secrets regarding individuals in or out of his own society. Ratting on a cop is just as serious a crime as ratting on your best friend. "They got to make a buck," says Danny. "They're human, too."

His philosophy, strangely enough, has a very familiar ring. He has a keen mind and a most engaging personality. He loves kids, and kids love him. They bring to him that loyalty which all children bring to those they admire. Here is food for thought. Danny himself, although he has never pondered the matter, was "taken" as a child. He is one of ten children. Chance placed him on the lower East Side. He looked up to and admired and gave loyalty to the "big shots" of the neighborhood, who liked him because he was "a nice, fresh little kid," who flattered him because it was their nature to flatter, and who allowed him to carry their guns. He grew up in their company, copied their manners, learned their code. Then chance gave him his first break. He was successful. He tried again, how many times I don't know. Finally, he was caught. "Don't never trust a cop," his friends had told him. "Don't never rat." "Come clean," the cops told him, "you're a nice kid. We'll see that you get a suspended sentence." Danny came clean. "Now tell us about so and so," said the cops. But that Danny would not do. His friends were his friends. Ratting was ratting. He shut up like a clam although he took plenty of punishment for his silence.

When finally his case came to trial he got the works, even though the cops had promised a suspended sentence. The truth of his underworld philosophy was brought home to him in a manner he would never forget. When he came out of Elmira twenty-two months later the code had become a religion. Every memory of his prison life had brought the thing more forcibly home. "Don't never trust a cop."

Today it would be worse than useless to try and make him acknowledge any social contract. In his final chapter, "Why I Won't Work," he shows us the futility of any such aspirations. If we take his case as typical, and I see no reason why we shouldn't, we have a very neat example of the way in which recruits and new leaders are made for the underworld. Ahearn shows us clearly, although entirely unconsciously, the futility of trying to reform anyone who, with a background such as his, has successfully engaged in crime before his first conviction.

Here indeed we have a problem for society. Its roots go deep into the foundations of the underworld, into the police departments of our largest cities, into society itself. And society must eventually meet it.

It is my intention in this introduction to defend neither the author nor his practices. Ahearn would resent it. He offers no apology, no justification, no defense. He is what he is. He has been through the mill. He carries the mute testimony of twelve bullets that meant business. But he has come out whole. In his own circles he stands high. He has friends throughout the country. It is easy, under such circumstances, to make the best of things.

This book is entirely his—"written", as previously explained, before two witnesses. Parts of it have been rearranged, parts of it cut to make it conform to public taste; but every word of it is Danny's.

J. S. C.

Chapter 1
THE CRIMINAL CREDO

What's the use of fighting for a woman when you can fight for money?

I hate a woman. Whenever she would ask me where you get your money, I would say: "Don't ask me where I get my money. I am a bootlegger or gambler." I know you can't trust a woman because they are with you today and someone else tomorrow, and then they may come back to you the next day. My motto is never to fool around with a broad or a regular broad. I always avoid such people, as the best you can get with them is plenty of trouble. Anybody that trusts a woman is out of his head, because they are with you today and when you are broke they are with someone else tomorrow. And then they fall in love—what I mean is passionate love not true, true love. I know in my own case I would never trust a woman. There's not a woman living that can say she ever heard anything from my lips. The best they can say for me is what they think.

Any man that kills a woman is out of his mind. Why should he go to jail for a lousy bum, when he can go outside and pick up another one?

Same thing—I don't feel friendly towards any cop. I won't say I don't like them. Some are regular and some are no good. A regular cop, I mean, is a fellow that won't look to frame me, and if he does catch you he will speak you out. Sometimes a cop takes money, like the guy that's a business man. You yourself can't do business with them. You got to get somebody else to do business for you. If you fool around long enough in this racket, you get to know them. They are known as fixers. It is a business.

In the underworld there is no such thing as friends, because everybody is trying to do the other. Friendship lasts as long as money is being made, but as soon as money runs out and there is no more money to be made, naturally, right there and then friendship ceases. They break—what is called a split—and they split away and they go where the money goes. The only way a gang can be powerful, the only way a mob sticks to each other, I won't

23

say die for each other, because it is a case of money with some of them.

I got friends in my heart, fellows that I used to have plenty of business with, but have no business with them at the present time, but they are in my heart because I know I am in their heart.

There are about twenty-five good mobs in New York. I do not run with them. With me it is a case where I'm a friend to all and don't look to settle myself with one mob, because maybe trouble starts and somebody is my friend. Why should I want to go and kill a friend of mine for nothing? But if I get to like somebody, and he happens to be with some good fellows, I will step for him without him knowing it. I never look for no glory, I was always a fellow that looked to make money.

The people I am with are good people and they're no double-crossers. I know I'm tangled up with good fellows, which has been proven to me as to several of my arrests. They stepped in and got bail. I have good connections myself, too. A connection is anybody that can help you, like a bondsman, a cop, an inspector, a lawyer, all money people, etc. You got to have plenty good connections in this racket.

There are some guys who are just with you to make that buck. They are out for that buck while they are with you, but if they can make more with the other side, they'll leave you and go with the other guy. If trouble starts, he may be your worst enemy. What I mean, make money, is to go out and steal or go and gamble. I never looked to make money with any mobs. To be truthful, I never made money with a mob, and if I did make money it was this here way, because with a mob I always got a pinch and it would cost me twice as much to get out. A pinch would come. I was always hard lucky in getting picked up and getting pinched.

I don't believe in that mob stuff. To my opinion, three good men that is heart and heart to each other, and stick to each other, can overtake any mob, like a mob of fifteen or twenty. This way you watch yourself, and don't take any walks with anybody, and don't ever listen to any phone calls. You are never home to nobody but to only them two; and in case you want to go and clip somebody, you know you three are always together, where in a mob of fifteen or twenty there is jealousy between themselves. I never yet seen two thieves to be friends for ten years.

Take the legitimate person, he can be a friend for twenty-five years or maybe a lifetime, but in the underworld jealousy starts either through a woman or money or some other source. Gangs don't stick together very long anyway. Fellows look to split away. Some may be down on the lower East Side, they may be with good people down there, but happen to get introduced to good people in other cities or what is known as uptown. Here they figure: "Why the hell should I go out and steal, when I can get in with this here mob and make a buck without getting pinched? Why should I jeopardize my liberty going out stealing, when I can go and get a buck a better way?" In some cases friendship still goes on, but you know, when you are away, you are all punk, and when you are around it is: "Hello, how are you," and a good big handshake.

They always call me an Irishman with a Jewish head, because I can always meet them with a smile and say: "Hello, how are you." But I would never let none of them step over my head. What I mean is, to look to get too intimate with me, so as where they could do business with me in another respect; which I can prove and verify, as I broke away from what I consider one of the best mobs in New York City or in any part of the country; and ever since I left that mob I never trusted anybody but what I consider an old-time friend. What I mean, a fellow that I have known for years and years, and probably went to school with and known since my childhood days.

In some cases there are good fellows running around, who turn out to be good fellows. What I mean is, if you get introduced to somebody who may like you, and right away you might take to him. Naturally you will say: "We will meet some time again." You may meet another time, and a time after that. Then you will make a date some time, and probably go to a cabaret. You might say: "How's things?" and he'll say: "Not so good." If I take a liking to somebody, he can have my undershirt; which was always my downfall, as I always took a liking to somebody who turned out to hurt me.

I wouldn't work with a guy that's known as a punk or a rat. I hate them. There are plenty of them. The Police Department have them on their payrolls. I never yet met a cop liked a rat.

Sometimes—which is known in the underworld—a cop will say: "He's a rat." I would look to find out for myself, because generally you can't believe the copper. He's looking to steam somebody else up.

A rat deserves to be dead. He deserves to be in the dirt, buried face down, so if he ever comes to life again he will go deeper and deeper.

The cop is your enemy, but you always have to use diplomacy. Why should I look to get myself in wrong with the cops? Because it don't pay and because they tell one another: "That son of a bitch, and so and so, he opened up on me." If you got a record, the Judge is prejudiced. Maybe he is more tougher than the cop is that gave it to you. Well, they don't trust you and, in fact, your own friends don't trust you when you squeal on a cop. Those cry-baby bandits that squealed on the cops—they all wound up in the can with plenty of time.

There's a lot of guys has plenty of guts, but what's the good of going in and sticking up a party with a couple of good fellows with you—when you get caught they are going to open up. That guy should go to work, because the racket calls for you to take what's coming. That's the only way you can gain friendship, and the only way you can get people's confidence.

One thing I wouldn't do is squeal on the cops, although there are a lot of guys that would, and in some cases they are lucky in getting out; but on the other hand you ain't going to benefit in squealing on the cop, because he always has an alibi, and there's nobody around when he's beating you up. Although it's an open book that a confession don't come from a man's mouth without being forced to it, because anybody with a little sense will always figure, it's better to be out on the street breathing that air than being in a can. I wouldn't squeal on any cop, which ain't in me to be a rat. Squealing on anybody is being a rat.

My motto is always to keep your bowels open and your mouth shut.

Once you start to talk, you ain't hurting anybody but yourself—as in a case of murder, what has been said is used against you. In another case you might get the minutes changed.

Ten minutes after an arrest the District Attorney is down looking to question you. If he's a tough nut, he might park himself outside and the bulls will look to force a confession out of you by bulldozing and calling you foul names. They'll give you a smack on the chin, and pull out jacks, and tell you what they're going to do to you—this and that. They generally do hit some poor chump that they know they can't do no business with, and if it's a hot case of murder, like killing a girl. Everybody is prejudiced against him in a case like that. People themselves would like to hurt the prisoner. If the cops do beat him and he is brought into court, they are tickled.

I have seen a case of a Filipino who was getting burned with cigars on the face, and after his face started to heal up they looked like quarter pieces, as the burns from the cigar just looked like the actual size of a quarter piece. This guy went to the chair, too.

When I was held on a murder charge, the bulls come over and said: "You, you dirty son of a bitch"—calling me all kinds of foul names, which I had one thing in my mind: "You can't kill me, and I ain't talking." They were bulldozing me and gave me a couple of smacks in the mouth. They seen their questioning did no good, they got disgusted and quit.

There's all kinds of people. Take the case of a Chink. I pity the white guy that's caught killing a Chink, because he's going to do a lot of explaining, and he's going to get convicted. Because the Chinks is going to get together all over the country to combine to stop them fights. They want to find out how these murders are getting committed. They know that white guys are doing these murders.

One thing, it's always good to take these Chinks out and give them a chance. Them Chinks ain't no rats. I never yet knew a Chink that would open up on anybody. When it comes to them getting questioned, they couldn't speak English, which would bring down their interpreters. I myself got offered money for to kill an interpreter, a Chink. I was going to do it, but got advised not to do it. I got told: "It will cost you ten times more than you can get, and don't listen to it." Them people I consider good friends of mine in that case.

I ain't saying I ever worked with Chinks, but I know plenty of them around the lower East Side. First of all, people are under the impression that Chinks kill Chinks, but I tell you, between you and I, that a Chink ain't got that much brains as to plan out them kind of murders that are committed, because a Chink is too God damn' dumb to scheme out a thing like that of killing a man.

For a man to commit murder, he's got to have no heart. Some fellows drop dead when they kill someone. A Chink—take a case of killing a woman—they are noted to give up all kinds of dough to be with a white woman. In some cases the white woman takes advantage of him and insults him, maybe. In a closed place, where nobody seen him commit murder, maybe he would cut her throat while she is asleep.

As far as a Chink is concerned, he ain't got that kind of brains as to figure out a murder like that. Generally, Chinks are very shrewd. I mean, where the people are that's got money. They scheme out, and get themselves connected with a party that they have faith in and can trust, knowing that that fellow has been maybe arrested; until one day he approaches him and propositions him about killing a Chink.

Some guys are in with these Chinks. They ain't got any guts to kill a Chink. They go and make a price with the Chink, and then go to a guy and proposition him to kill a Chink, and that's how they make money. I consider him a smart guy, because the guy that commits a murder like that is a God damn' fool. I ain't going to let any guy get any money on me. I ain't going to play ball with those guys. Let him go out and take a chance, too.

The people come to you and make connection with you, and when it comes to the money, you want to see the dough on the line. Naturally, they bring you to this Chink and it's talked over, and he asks: "How much?" They guarantee a good lawyer, and they stick right with you to the end.

I got brought before one of the leading Chinks and propositioned, where the money was going to be put up on the line, and when I asked for a said amount, he said: "That's a lot of money." I said: "What the hell do you want?" He says: "This here guy's fooling me. I can have a Chink shipped in"; and a Chink gets 800 for killing a leader, and so much for killing a small Chink, like a laundry guy. I says: "I know too much about what's going on, as I come right from that vicinity." I know a lot of Chinks in this country.

The white fellows kill them. It ain't dangerous to kill them, it's the after effects—the tong wars. Them guys that kill the Chinks are punks that don't know better. But there is guys that do kill them Chinks. There's big money being paid out all right, but the second hand gets it, and he gives the third hand maybe a thousand dollars. Maybe he's getting ten or twenty thousand for killing the Chink. He's sort of a murder agent.

I'll trust nobody. They can do business with me this way, that is, give me a tip; but I won't work with them, that is, go in and do the job.

Take the Irish—they are all too hot-headed. Ninety percent of the Irish fellows, they get drunk. They ain't noted to make money, and they'll only hurt their best friends. As far as making money, they don't know how to make it, unless they're lucky. They generally look to work, or do foolish things where they get more time than when wide open. They never use their heads.

I happen to be a different nationality to them people around my section, and if they can say one wrong word against me as far as money is concerned, or as far as respect is concerned, I will smoke a boloney. I'm no bulldozer and won't bother nobody. The biggest bum can come over to me and say: "Have you got the price of a cup of coffee?" I find myself saying to them: "Do you want to eat, fellow?" If I was in a place eating, and see another fellow that hasn't got anything to eat, I can't eat; that would hurt me. I would always look to be generous enough to give up half of what I always got.

Take a Jewish fellow. There's good ones and bad ones.

I wouldn't say I won't work with an Irish fellow. I worked with plenty. I just avoid Irish fellows in my neighborhood, because what they don't know about me don't hurt them. I never do no business with them.

Negroes, Italians and Greeks, they're all alike to me. I wouldn't work with a nigger the same as a white man. When I go

Chapter 3
HOW TO STICK UP A FUR JOINT

Some fur stores carry nearly $100,000 worth of furs in their window. They are just like money, the same as diamonds are. A good fellow with a good head on him, he knows he can take from a needle to an anchor and always get rid of it.

The best time to hit a fur joint is in the winter when there's snow on the ground, or a good rainy day when it's cold. Cops that are on beat watch them places more than any other places of business.

There's a certain store in Brooklyn—the second largest fur store in New York—where it has two entrances. It's the biggest fur store in Brooklyn. It's much like a public place. Anybody can walk in, but today they got it so that they have their doors locked, and if they don't know you and you look suspicious to them, they are all set with them buttons to give an alarm.

The best way to work would be to have two cars. You need five fellows in your mob. You need three fellows to do the stuff, and two chauffeurs. Take yourself a couple of big sacks, big burlaps bags. Don't think you can run in and out, to go back again. You can just make that one lap. You can't waste too much time.

Here's my opinion how to beat that joint. The best time of day is nine o'clock in the morning, just at the opening hour, as it's pretty dead, people are into their business already. You work with two cars, which stay right in front of one of the entrances. They're waiting for you before you get there.

Two employees open that store, and after they get in they lock the doors. One entrance is on this block and the store runs through one street to the other—through the block. About sixty feet from the corner. You park the cars around the corner, both cars on one entrance. You pick out the spot where's the best getaway.

These two men step in to open that place. Wait until they have all the vaults open, because in that place they got about six big vaults full of furs. I have seen the vaults and have seen the display. The display alone is something like $150,000 worth. You can see the vaults from the street, and if somebody comes in to buy a coat they don't sell a coat from the window but take a coat out of the vault. The vaults have racks inside and the coats are on the racks.

I can tell how to judge furs. But to tell you the truth, I know I got a feller that's in that racket—the fur line—and he just knows how much an article is worth by looking through that window. I take him for a walk one day and ask: "Do you think that stuff is worth so much?" And he tells me, yes or no. There's a lot of phony furs around, but the big places like that is reliable.

Here's how you get the lay. You get yourself a girl. She don't have to know nothing, because it's very foolish to trust a girl. You tell her: "Come on, kid, if I see a good buy on a coat, I'll buy you a coat. I seen a nice coat in this place and if it looks good on you I'll buy it for you." You go there and look at that coat. In the meantime I am observing every move is being made there, see how the vaults are, if the inner door is locked or open, because you can't work on a blind on that kind of job. You don't like anything they show you, or else it's too much money, and you walk out. They don't know nothing.

Now you know the whole layout. Generally the guy that goes to see that kind of thing is a good head, and people have confidence in him and listen to what he says. You watch and see what time they open up them vaults in the morning and see who closes it, and see if they put all the stuff in there at night. Generally around them vaults is a sign above the vault, "Holmes Protection." You can't crack them vaults open, although I had friends that blew open the vaults of a big New York company four years ago—that five million dollar robbery.

You wait for the other people that is working in the place to come. After that the store is wide open. The door is kept closed but not locked. When the people come, like an employee, they open the door and let him in and close and lock it again. When they open up both doors, that's the time the leader goes in.

Naturally, you all can't step in at once. You have what is called a leader and he goes in first, and he lingers around for just about a minute or two until the others step in. He steps in first for this reason—as to their getting into the place—what is known, to make an entrance. After everybody is in, everybody gets hoisted up in the air, and you take all the coats out of there.

You got it all planned for you to get into the joint, and you know the people is there that you want, so you go stick up the doorman and he puts the O.K. on you. In you go, and stick up everybody; but don't look to hurt anybody, if possible. Relieve them all of their jewelry, and thank them, and walk out.

Right outside of Chicago, recently, guys walked in and stuck up a joint—seven guys stuck up a big night club—made a little girl get out and entertain them. After that they made the band play, and they thanked the boss and thanked the people.

Some fellows I know did the job of blowing up the vaults of a big New York corporation. They had good reliable information from the watchman that worked there, that there was five million dollars' worth of furs. He was a good fellow and a nervy guy. They observed everything. It was in a nice section, where it's dead and people not walking in the streets. These people are not protected by Holmes Protection, because they had a watchman there. That was the inside man for these guys. They observed that building and planned it out, but what was the good of all their planning, when one guy already told his girl all about the trick. Six of them got pinched. They had two big Bulldog Mack trucks to carry away the stuff. No guns was used, except in firing at the cops. Every time they went to the building, the bulls was always trailing them, until they got together one night and planned: "We are going on Sunday afternoon. We will have to ship in the acetylene in the morning."

They opened them vaults with acetylene torches. They worked on them vaults for a good couple of hours. As you know, the cops always look to try to get you dead to rights. They had a couple of vaults blew open already when the cops came up and they started firing shots, and these fellows fired back at them. About two hundred shots was exchanged in the fight. They surrounded this place with 250 cops. Nobody got away. The trucks got away and the drivers got away with them. I guess they were rented from a truckman who would put up an alibi that they got stolen.

When the cops got into the place, they knew the fellows, because they were known as good safecrackers. They shot one fellow in both knees. They said: "Stick them up and lay down on the floor with your arms straight out." As he did, the cop happened to shoot and happened to break both kneecaps. Another fellow, they broke his jaw and he's got gold wire in his jaw today. They gave them a severe beating and took them to Bellevue Hospital. There was three of them in real bad shape. The other guys got beaten and kicked.

They took them to Police Headquarters and booked them, but in this case the fellow that was shot in both knees lay in Bellevue Hospital a long while. When a man is a prisoner in a hospital, they look to get rid of him quick. Anyway, he got sent down to the Tombs, held without bail, as he was a third offender in this State of New York. He already put in about five bits throughout the country. He got sentenced to four years in Sing Sing. He did it in about two and a half. Naturally it cost a lot of money for that case.

The watchman let them in. He was sent up too. They made believe they tied him up. They did tie him up, but only to make it look good. But you know, in a case like that they make a thorough investigation, and they saw he wasn't any too efficiently tied up, and they put two and two together until he broke down. Although nobody ratted in the case, but they didn't stick to each other as far as money was concerned. The guys that got out didn't look to take care of the other guys that were still in. One guy got ten years; the others got five and four years, like that.

That job went wrong account of the girl squealing. This broad rang up the cops and told the cops about how this here New York corporation is going to get robbed. They were pretty clever fellows and daring sons of bitches, but one guy happened to confide in his girl. He told her: "Don't worry, after this here, I'm going to go in business and go straight." I don't know what happened to the girl. I haven't seen her from that day to this.

You clip a diamond salesman and you make money. A man who travels on the road never carries less than fifty thousand dollars' worth of stuff—diamonds. Here's how he does his business. When a man goes out on the road, it's no cash with him. He looks to walk into a jewelry store and puts out his displays. Sometimes you get a tip off his own boss. His own boss makes an agreement with you, saying: "I want ten percent," known as a tipster's end; but in a case where there's a lot involved, you look to give up fifteen percent, and he looks to buy back the stuff, giving you a good price, and he collects insurance.

To my opinion, them jewelry salesmen are the shrewdest guys and the hardest ones to get in contact with to throw up—stick up. What I mean by that is, they are always in fear, figuring that somebody may have suspicions about them. Or maybe somebody pointed him out, that he is a jewelry salesman. Whenever he's on the road, he's always looking in back of him, and if he sees the same face twice he walks over to a cop and stands by a cop. Naturally, if he sees the same face again, he goes to another cop and he tells the cop who he is. This may cause a pickup.

There is only one way to trail him—to have plenty of money on your person. Let one man carry the guns in a brief case, with wire and tape, and probably one or two pairs of handcuffs. You carry wire and tape so you can tie him up and put tape on his mouth. Adhesive tape.

You treat these guys gently—you got to. If he is a Jew, you call him an Irish son of a bitch; and if he is an Irishman, you call him a Jew bastard.

Suppose you are a jewelry guy. I know you got the stuff on you. It's a good idea to send one man after him all the way one time, and he trails him right back to where he came from. You get a good line on him. The next time out you make the same points with him. Be dressed very neat, and one man sits in the same car with him and the others sit in the following coach. If you have a chance to clip him or stick him up on the train, O.K. Naturally, when they get on the train they disguise themselves. They might wear a soft hat on their way out.

To hoist them downtown in Maiden Lane is pretty tough. It's like walking into jail.

While riding on the train they generally carry the stuff around their neck. No man that's out on the road never carries it in grips. They generally always step out with stuff valued at enormous amounts, and they have the stuff around their neck in pouches.

Maybe you get a tip that he has a hundred to two hundred thousands' worth of stuff. You got to use your head to get the drop on him. He ain't going to look to holler, because he is afraid to get killed. He knows the stuff is insured. They look to save their life, and later they report it to the police.

A good way to clip him is, don't let him get a chance to go to a hotel. Say he is going to a city like Chicago. Maybe he drinks water on the train—see if you can poison the water on the train. If anybody else steps up, like an innocent person, you tell them the water is no good, and you avoid them from drinking it.

Another good way is when he is leaving the station. Generally they never look to walk the streets, because they're always in fear. Seize the best way when he steps off the train. Maybe he must go to a toilet in the station. If so, walk right in behind him. If there's a porter, stick him up also. If the porter has a key, take the key, lock them both in and break the key in the lock.

Another good way, if he jumps into a cab you slide right in behind him and tell him: "Shut up—keep your mouth shut, you son of a bitch! I'll kill you!" Naturally, he may look to make a holler. In that case your friends slip into another cab right behind you. You keep riding until your friends come up. They cut you off and send you in to the sidewalk. I hoist the driver of the cab I am in. We pull out the handcuffs and tie them up, handcuff them to bars inside the taxicabs, and take the stuff and beat it.

Generally you have a connection in the said city where you are pulling the trick, so you can lay over for a couple of days without ever going out in the street, and have your meals brought in. Nobody is going to know what's happened, only the person where you are at. Naturally, you take care of him by staking him to some money.

The best way to get away from the city is for the guy with the stuff, let him go by himself. Then you follow, probably separating and taking different railroads into the city where you came from.

In them cases, if you hoist a diamond guy for a hundred thousand dollars, the papers come out with two hundred thousand robbery. Sometimes it's an insurance racket.

I tell you truthfully that the only way a thief can get a tip as to what you got on your person or what you are doing, is through your own friends. Because people that don't know you, they don't know what you are doing.

Supposing you are in Cleveland. You know a jeweler there. He gives me a tip in a business way that you got ten thousand on you. How do I know you got it on you, unless he tells me?

Another good way is to make friendship with somebody in the jewelry line, that has a jewelry store and has salesmen coming in to him all the time. He gives you a tip. He says: "You know so and so, a guy comes to my store maybe once a week or once a month on such a day, and he's got a lot of stuff." You look to find out how much stuff he's got. You take his word, because he's in the business. Most of them jobs are pulled off by that kind of information.

Chapter 5
THE AUTOMOBILE RACKET

The first step in stealing a car, I would make connection with what is known as a fence for automobiles. He tells me: "I'll give you two hundred for such and such a car, and five hundred for another kind of a car." The fences are located right in the city here, usually. Sometimes they are out of town, sometimes they are in the city. They are all over. I just drive it right to the place, and I get my money. Right on the spot.

I know the price of all makes of cars I am supposed to get, but he wants one particular kind, knowing he can make the numbers better than on other kinds. Fords and Buicks are the best, because they're so common when it comes to be identified. You always try to get a dark color.

I go out with a car, have another fellow with me. He drives me around until I see a good car. When I see somebody step out, I step in. Sometimes they leave the key in, and if not I open it with a knife. I feel it with my hand and I just know how to turn them ignition locks.

Sometimes the transmission is locked. If you race the gas real hard, and all of a sudden you throw in the clutch, you can force the car and break the lock. Also there is the ground wire on a car. The wires go right in from the ignition. You pick up the hood and just disconnect the ground wire, and put another piece of wire there. You then make a connection and that starts the car for you. Then there's a door lock. When there's a door lock, you can pry the door lock open with a jimmy. It's best to look for a car that's open.

The best place to steal cars is anywhere and wherever you see a good car. I would steal one on 48th Street and Fifth Avenue, or on Broadway or on Riverside Drive, because that's where good cars are. Good residential sections is generally where you get good cars.

You have to steal new cars. If I can steal it without the fellow seeing it, I will take it. If he steps over to me while I am stealing it, I will just say I made a mistake. People on the street see you jumping in the car. They figure it's your own car.

Here's how they work back the mileage meter. It's an open book, when you go to buy a Rolls-Royce car, that the Rolls-Royce people won't let it out on the street unless 500 miles is on the mileage meter. They have what is known as a driveway, which is a stationary block, where the wheels just turn but the car doesn't move.

You change the mileage from 20,000 to 8,000 miles just with emery wheels, and they just turn back the mileage. Here's the stationary driveway, the wheels keep turning around and the meter turns back. You put an emery wheel right in the mileage clock, right inside of the speedometer. While the wheels is going forward, when it reaches to the mile that the speedometer is going to register, when it's just about to register, you just yank it right back and that throws back the mileage. Or you can take off the speedometer and break the glass, and turn back the mileage that way and put a new glass on. Another thing, you can put a new speedometer on, if you wish, and run it like the Rolls-Royce people do for 500 miles or whatever mileage you want, without having the car on the street.

This fence, he takes it off my hands and he pays me. If you want to sell the car yourself, there is more money in it. I can go and be my own salesman, and tell a fellow: "Do you want to buy a Buick?" He says: "How much? Bring me a Buick and I will buy it." You go out and steal a Buick or a nice car. The next move is you want to get them numbers changed. Sometimes they are on the crank case, sometimes right on the block of the motor. About this plate on the inside of the dashboard, you take that off and get another one made. They cost you the same as they would cost anybody else—you go to a die place, and they make you one.

About selling the car and getting the license plates and the ownership license—here's how it's worked. You go and take yourself a little ride, or walk if you wish to, and go to what is known as junk shops, where they sell old cars that are going to be ditched for junk. You may see a motor there. Sometimes in empty lots you see an automobile that's discarded. You go over and see what the number is on the block, or wherever the said number is going to be. You mark it down on a slip of paper. I know that every car has a secret number, but I don't know where it is. That's a secret that is known to only one man of the automobile company itself. I don't say you can fix a secret number, but I hear of cases where they do fix secret numbers, and they work with the man that knows the secret number. Sometimes it might be in the chassis of the car, or probably in the body of the car.

Here's how you get the license for the car, to make people believe that you own the car. Naturally, the fellow you are going to sell to wants to see an owner's license. You go up to the License Bureau, fill yourself out an application and just hand it in. But I know today, before you can get a license, you got to have a bill of sale from the person you are buying it. I am talking about a few years ago, when they didn't ask for no bill of sale.

Although, you can make a connection to get a bill of sale with an automobile place—what is known as a second-hand automobile place. Anyway, you get the license, and you get yourself a phony bill of sale. You try to make a connection with an automobile store, or probably you might have a friend in there, or know somebody for to get you a couple of their blank bill of sales. You have somebody else fill them out, and have a notary seal put on there for a quarter. Never give your right name—always a fictitious name when getting out a license and on the bill of sale. Everything must correspond.

You steal up to the fellow and sell him the car. He pays you. You don't see him any more, he don't see you. He may ride around for a long while with the said car without getting caught.

Another way to get numbers off cars is to go down to the export piers and, as you know, they do a lot of exporting of cars. Generally, there's the whole dimensions and everything on the case—the motor number, probably the body number, and every other thing that you would want. You know the car is going to South America or to Europe—that is a good move. Whoever's shipping that car just knows where that motor car has gone to, which can be traced.

The best idea I know of, is to go to what is known as a dead car that's being piled in for junk, because the manufacturer doesn't know what's happened to that car. You note down that number.

You get yourself dies made up. They ain't too expensive, and you get all kinds of numbers made, and plates; like Buicks, they have plates on the dashboard and a number on the block. Anybody that knows that racket knows what kind of stuff he needs. He needs the dies and a torch. You don't do that yourself. You make a connection with a good mechanic who knows that kind of stuff. He charges anywhere from $50 to $75 for doing that sort of thing. He chisels off that number. You don't see where it has been done—you don't always have to take the whole number off. Out of an O you can make an 8 and out of a 9 you can make an 8. You might only have to change one number on the whole lot.

You always have to have the number that is on a Buick on another Buick, but you can put any number on. Maybe you get caught, but the guy that is going to be pinched, he's got a bill of sale and everything he wants. A lot of guys get pinched with stolen cars, but they don't know they are stolen. They may get into an accident some time, and the Automobile Squad may be on hand, and they can tell whether a number has been changed. They take this guy down and lock him up for grand larceny, for stealing an automobile. The guy makes a holler and says he bought it. To them it's always an alibi—they don't believe the guy. He gets bailed out and at Court time the guy obtains a counselor if he can do so. If not, he always produces the bill of sale. If he's got a good record, ninety-nine chances out of a hundred he's going to get out.

These fences that have cars, they generally run second-hand joints. Generally they're good mouthpieces—they got a good tongue and can gain your confidence in selling you a car, just like an ordinary salesman. In some cases they ship them cars and export them themselves to foreign countries, and get the same price as an automobile company would for their own car. They probably would change the body over. They take and just switch the bodies—like if you bring in a car with a maroon body on it, they might take the body off and put a blue one on. They have people working there that don't know what's going on, the same as a legitimate automobile place would have. They believe they are working for a legit concern. The fellow who changes the numbers, he's in the know. Maybe the Automobile Squad might know them people, too. Maybe they pinched them some time or other, and they work with the cops in some cases. The cops know what's going on and they get seen, and they just don't bother.

To do a stickup, it's a good idea you should steal a car. Leave it in some spot as long as you know you are going to get away. You go and steal a pair of license plates, try to get to a place known as a dead storage, where people leave cars for months, and you know the plates ain't going to be missed. You don't go out and steal plates until the last minute, because plates are reported, and to me, anybody stealing them plates shouldn't do so until the last minute, because them plates are reported just like a stolen car. They are known as hot plates, and although you can go to the toughest sections, toughest thoroughfares, where there are plenty of cops, no one would know the worst of it. Sometimes you can leave a car right outside of Police Headquarters and it won't be found, and you can go there and steal a car.

One thing I know, the best next move is to make a connection with a garage to keep the stolen car. Today you can't make no connection with garages, because today they have the Automobile Squad, and they ride around to all of these garages during the night and check up on all said cars. Another thing, when you drive a car to a public garage today, the owner of the garage takes down the license number, and he telephones the number to Police Headquarters. If the car is stolen, then they know where the car is. You don't know when the Automobile Squad is coming around to check up on the garage. Although I know of a case where a stolen car lay in a garage for three weeks. They just didn't happen to find it.

When a car is stolen, the police are notified and they notify all the garages. The garage owner is supposed to take down all numbers and telephone them in to the Police or keep a check of them. Maybe at midnight he telephones in all that came in up to that hour. That's why they take down your license number today. They keep them as a record, but today you can send anybody for your car.

Another thing is, you can't all go to the garage. The only thing to do is to have one man go to that garage and get that car. He's the chauffeur, and he's the one that goes out to steal the car.

When you steal a car for a stickup, steal it some time before you do the stickup. You can steal it a couple of weeks ahead of time. A fellow with any kind of a head never rides in a stolen car, except to get away. You can go and get yourself a private garage out in a nice residential section, where they would be surprised it's going to be. You go and rent yourself a garage out in Borough Park or Flatbush, where people own their own houses and have private garages on their property. They are tickled to death to accommodate you in that way. But sometimes, if you aren't connected, the party might get suspicious, and seeing you not taking the car out for a week they will telephone the cops themselves. The cops will find it a stolen car and take it themselves. It always pays to work a connection, where you ring a party if you are going to take out that car today. You always work with a party, and you ring that party up and say: "Hello, this is so and so. Listen, was anybody around the garage since the time the boiler is in there?" He says: "Nobody has been around." Naturally you say: "I'm going to take it out." He always gives you the information as to who's been around, and if nobody's been around you take out the car and put on phony plates and go. You don't leave that car in the garage with the license plates that belong to it, but you always put on another pair.

If you wait until the end to steal a car just before you do a stickup, you will wind up with nothing. Luck may turn against you. It's always a good idea to do these things ahead of time, to be prepared, because everything turns on you in the end.

Here is another way to make a buck in the automobile racket. There is the phony tire game. A guy steps up to you with brand-new-looking tires. The tire you would throw away from your automobile, that is sold to a junky, who sells it to a place where they make a new tire out of that old tire with tar and very little rubber, by mixing the tar with the rubber, and they have a die there to make the tread of a known tire, like a Goodyear or Goodrich Silvertown Cord, but the lining of the shoe don't look so new, so they put powder in there. You think you are getting a buy, and you get taken that way. They are wrapped up in paper, just like they would have a tire in a reliable tire store. They just show you one part of that tire by tearing the paper off. You see it's new and think it's new.

You take it home and put it on your car. You will ride all right with it for probably about fifty miles, and then it will get a blow out on it. You take it to a vulcanizer and he will tell you how you got stuck.

Them tires is bought for the sum of $4.00 from the man that fixes them up, known as a tire plant. This is a big place which is like any other big tire manufacturer. He has all the dies, and he is located in a spot, and he don't look to trust everybody but only the people he sells to. He just knows who he is selling to.

Chapter 6
THE POLITICAL RACKET

I will tell you one thing, in order to get in with big politicians you have to be recommended very, very good. They don't look to bother with every Tom, Dick and Harry. They don't look to work with local fellows, but with fellows that are strangers to them.

A certain politician wants a fellow out of the way. He lives in San Francisco. So he has a connection here in New York, and sends word to this connection in New York to send on a couple of good guys, generally three to four men. In a case like that it is not a case of money, but you can get in on things. He'll tell you that if so and so gets elected, he will see that you get favors—gambling, etc. I know for myself I ask for $50,000, but he says he cannot give up money, but will give me concessions of either crap games or card games or clearing house numbers on the Stock Exchange. That's a good proposition, and you can make a lot of money that way, but it's always best to do on a cash basis, although in 90 cases out of 100 you never get cash. So you fix it up and tell him O.K.

The next thing you have to do, if he is going to meetings, etc., you have to trail along with him. Maybe somebody is looking to hurt him. You act not only as a means to getting somebody else rid of, but as a bodyguard as well. You all go around together.

The next thing you do, you go around to polls. They know the tough districts, where they think the men want to get votes. You have to talk to people. You walk up and tell the voters: "Vote for so and so." You try to put fear into them, but try and talk to them in a nice manner. Sometimes them people don't do as you tell them to. They promise you, and then they turn on you.

You work with the cops. Say it is a tough joint. That politician, if he has any connection, will pull a connection with the cops. And you walk into the joint, grab the boxes, steal the votes, throw them down the sewer, etc. It's been done many times, and gets in the papers. You steal the votes and tear them up. The party that is in has always got the power of that city. You always work with cops. You get to be known as a floater. You can vote ten times yourself without being recognized, because if a party does not show up to vote on election day you vote for him anyway, and if there is anybody there on the opposite side, like a poll watcher, he is afraid that he will get hurt, and keeps his mouth shut. Or else you try to buy out the other side.

In them elections it winds up with plenty shooting matches. The other side hires guys too. They don't want to give in. It leads to a lot of trouble. When the party is in, if he don't live up to what he has promised to do for you, you hurt him. You wind up sticking him up, or probably killing him. You cannot commit murder with him outright. You put a bomb in his car or in his house. They generally work with dynamite, putting it in the starter of the car, to get a politician out of the way.

They promise that they will do everything for you, and when the party is in, they forget you. They tell you: "I am for the people, with the people, and to hell with the people." That is my opinion. But mostly when that party is in they are O.K., and you can do a lot of favors helping fellows to get on the police force, etc., and it's always done. You can get any favor you want, because him, knowing that you have it on him, cannot turn you down, fearing that you might talk. He might also give me a concession on what is known as mooning—moonshine. Them speakeasies, they cannot buy their alcohol from anybody but me. If they don't buy from me, their place gets closed up by cops. The cops pinch them.

I know one thing, if a fellow is a good friend of mine, if he tells me that he got fined $100, I would get that back for him. You get your fines back through the city. It's taken off the books—they fix the books up. Fellows get caught with guns there. They have no Sullivan Law in some parts of the Middle West. If you have a gun on your person and get caught, they lock you up and take the gun away from you, and if you have no one to go to the front for you, they fine you $25. I know of cases where a fellow got his gun back and his fine back.

Cops know that. If you are in solid, they will look to help you, because they know that you can break them. They figure you can do them a big favor. Sometimes them cops they can't be good to everybody. A fellow might be drunk. A cop might not like his mush.

That fellow might come up to me, knowing that I am connected pretty good. The cops are bothering him. I have to go to the front for him, and I can use him to do me a favor some other time. Through him I will make the money. He will probably hurt somebody for me. That is the only favor he can do for me. I walk over to the cop and say: "Leave so and so alone"; or else I go to my friend, the politician, and I tell him. I have already seen a politician come down and bawl a cop out.

A politician wants another man put out of the way so that he can get in. Sometimes you might not be working direct, like with the Mayor, because that man has got people. The big politicians themselves are not in office. That party may be on the side with the Mayor. The Mayor is just his mouthpiece. Him and the Mayor has a big talk, and he gets a proposition. Anything he wants he gets. By him getting it you get it.

People put you up in office, and they don't stick together, get into arguments, and turn on each other. They have what is known as a split. Then they go with someone else. I know of a case in the West where a party is the present Mayor, and he was a former Supreme Court Judge. He got a proposition to run for office as Mayor, knowing that they had a tough election, and that he probably would carry the city. The Judge got elected. After his first term, he ran for a second term. The politician who made him run for that office, was his opponent. That happens in the West.

I have seen a case where six fellows came from another city in the West and came into this city, not meaning New York, but I mean a certain city in the Middle West, and they came and went to this politician's house, called him out to the front door of his home, stuck him up with six guns, and made him walk. He knew where to walk them. He said: "We will walk up here and talk it over." Him knowing that we were all there, his bodyguard. We winded up shooting one of the men and getting my man away.

You try to pull a connection with the bodyguards on the other side. Maybe they might know somebody you know, and you would look to talk it over, work in with you; but if they won't listen, you wind up in shooting matches with them. You just look to steer them. If they are stopping in a hotel, sneak up and stick them up right in their rooms. They might do the same thing with you. That leads to shooting.

In Chicago in recent elections, when the Mayor got beat out, they had many hundred gunmen. On the day of election, the politician hires plenty local guys. But when it comes down to the shooting, he has them imported. But the other people are right around. They will hit you with a stick or something. When it comes to the actual shooting, they never trust the local fellow. They always have an imported man, knowing that nobody knows him in that city. A lot of people might know of him, and probably have seen him, but I mean that he is in disguise with the cops, and the politicians hardly know him.

You take in Chicago nowadays when politicians break with each other. During that election, there was plenty of shooting and plenty of money spent on that election, because he was pretty good towards the racket fellows and a thief, and towards gambling and all kinds of vice. They put up a lot of campaign money. The racket fellows themselves do it. They make their dollar the same way. They know if he gets defeated there will be another mob step in.

One of the biggest got out because he did not get what he wanted. The thieves themselves put up plenty of money to keep that man in office, because they know that they will make ten times as much if he gets elected, and they will see to it that he gets elected. That is their living. They commit murder for it. They will do things without him knowing it, probably. But it is going to help him. Like in the case where a fellow probably might kill somebody during an election. He knows that that fellow committed murder for him, and he will be well taken care of.

I happened to be walking with one of the leading politicians, and was drinking with him and a couple of captains. The cops were notified: "Don't bother this fellow or the fellows that he has with him," and I could walk in and get anything what I wanted in a prostitution house. I never look to get any of their money. You know what I mean. I happened to be walking with this politician and just coming out of a big auditorium. For that man I would have committed crime without a dime. He would lay out his cards on the table and tell it to you. I came out with him, and after drinking we happened to run into some people. He said to me:

"There is a guy who turned on me." He said that these people was probably coming to help him—vote for him in his election—and what happened, this fellow was right in with the Mayor, and was even more popular than the Mayor of that city. I mean my friend. And I know in my heart, whatever I would want from him I could get. I knew that if I killed a guy in that city I could get away with it.

He happened to get into an argument with this other guy, and there happened to be two cops standing there. He says: "Why are you so nice to me now? You bum, when I ran for office you looked to get the other guy elected." I jumped in and grabbed him by the throat. I said: "You see this, I'll put this in your eye." The cop said: "Kill that son of a bitch." I busted this guy around.

This friend of mine used to share the same office with another politician, they were pretty good friends. They were working together at one time, and they had what is known as a primary to get a man in office. They called me on the phone one day and told me quick to come down. There were a lot of cops outside, and they told us: "Get up in that office and break up the entire office." It was the politician's office. We sneaked up with cue sticks and started belting everybody in the place. We broke up his office, just because he turned. There was no money given up. We were offered different things—to get in on things.

I happened to go back to that said city a couple of months later, and I happened to go to the Judge's office, and I asked for so and so, meaning the other politician, my friend, that was sharing his office. He said: "He is not here no more and I don't talk to him. I would like you to work with me in this election. I want to get so and so out of the way." I said: "Put up $50,000 and I will do it"; but he didn't want to do it. He wanted to proposition me in different ways, what he would give me. I don't live on no promises with him. I went out, and he told me not to tell anybody.

But I had to tell this friend of mine, the other politician. He said: "That dirty bitch, he is no God damn' good. He will turn on you as he turned on me." I saw that he was right. The cops told me also. They said: "I would like to see him get killed." Maybe if I would have killed him they would have helped to convict me. I didn't have faith in any one of them cops. I didn't want business with them cops.

All on account of that jealousy I got shot. Here is how I got shot. Seeing that I came from another city, and seeing that I pushed in fellows that were with me, that made them sore. They figured if they got me out of the way that they would be in. They laid for me in another city. I happened to get into the city and I was coming out of a restaurant, and I saw this double-crossing politician, and I said: "What are you doing here?" He told me he was trying to get connected. If he would have asked me to get into a car with him I would have done it. We had a little talk. I called him a rat. He came back with a big gun in his hand and shot me. Who would have thought he would shoot me? I knew what it was all about. It was account of jealousy, seeing that he could not get in, and it kind of made him sore. And I guess he figured if he got me out of the way that he would get in.

He was just looking for reputation. If I would have harmed him in any way, I would not have blamed him. But he was just seeking a reputation, although he had several people come and talk to me to square it up. But I won't. I don't respect him in any way.

The cops knew I got shot on account of a political ring, but I would not give in. I happened to know and been in with one of the leading politicians in Cleveland, and been on parties with him, and the cops knew that. There was a big scandal going on throughout the city at that time, and a couple of leading politicians went to the State Prison of Ohio.

They like fellows out there that won't open up. As was in a case of mine right in Cleveland, where a secretary to a boxing commissioner and some of the leading politicians came to help to get me discharged. I couldn't say why they did that, they were all good fellows there. Sometimes strangers turn out to be very good friends for you. In New York it ain't done much.

I didn't know them, but they knew me. On the other hand, some of them didn't know me and I didn't know them, but they read about it in the papers and, naturally, they seen the way I was caught, that I just didn't give a God damn', as I was smiling all the ways through the case, badly bent over from bullets that I had received about five weeks before, and I was just out of the hospital. One thing, I wouldn't care if I was to get shot right now, and I had two minutes to live, and they brought the man before me that shot me, I would look to do him more good than harm. I would say: "No, that ain't the man," and tell them the guy got out the back window.

Landlords are easy money. I got a friend of mine who collects rents uptown. He's insured for that money. You work on this information. Say in an apartment house of 125 families, you know the rent is $150 a month. Some is in checks, but there is plenty cash. Or take a common ordinary landlord on the East Side. He wants cash. There is apartments around $80 and $90 a month. They get paid by cash. Here's a good way how to work it.

Maybe you yourself might live in the house, and you know on such and such a day this landlord comes for his rent. I know on that day I got to pay my rent—like the first of the month. I also know and find out the information as to the others—I find out they all pay on that day. I scheme out, and watch and see what he does. I give him a tail—which is known as a trail—and see what he does. Maybe he may go to a bank, or to another apartment house and collect too. If he goes to the next apartment house, don't give him a chance to get into an apartment, because probably he might live there, or maybe he might give it to a janitor for to make a deposit.

You watch him go all through it one month. Then, if he collects all the money before he deposits, you would wait until he collects all. That's how I would work it as to trailing him. If I saw he gave it to a janitor to deposit, I would watch the janitor. I would watch every move, and have a good line on him when that day came for me to stick him up. I would wait until he got through with all the apartments. I would wait for him downstairs, and stick him up, and take him and walk him up to the roof and strip him, because he may have a money belt on him, or may put it in his socks, because some landlords are very greedy and may do that, or he may put it in his shoes. It's no use to take five hundred when maybe you can get a thousand.

Take him up on the roof, treat him as nice as you can. Take his pants off and take his pants with you. That will avoid him from running down the stairs. Tell him: "You stay here for fifteen minutes, till I get away," because he might holler as you are going down the stairs—that is, if you work without tying him up. It's a much better idea to tie him up to the chimney on the roof, or something else, and put a piece of tape over his mouth and screw away.

Payrolls are easy money, too. Sometimes you might get a tip that there's a $20,000 payroll in such and such a joint. You work on that information that you get, and you watch every time how the money goes in—how long the people stay in there that deliver the money. What I mean is, today any concern that has a standing payroll, good size payroll, has what is known as an armored car bring their payrolls to them.

Them payrolls are made up by the bank in envelopes, as the firm would rather pay that few extra dollars, whatever it costs, and have the armored car service deliver them the money, instead of them sending a messenger, like a girl or man, to the bank for the payroll.

You find out if the armored car service, which in some cases pays off the men in the shop themselves, and when they have the payroll distributed to the workers then they leave. This is a good way to protect the payroll.

Then it may be a shop of maybe a hundred people. It don't pay to go up there and stick them all up and take the workers' salary. I believe if you got to steal, steal from the rich people that can afford it.

You get that information. Maybe you find out that the armored car service is to bring the money, and they leave it and get a receipt signed, and they go. When you see the payroll getting delivered, you watch that, and if it's in, say, a loft building, and the office is on the second floor where the payroll is going to, you know just where they're going to put the payroll. You watch every move, see how they pay off. See how they handle the money. See how long it stays before they distribute it to the workers. The next best move is to park yourself up on the floor above. Have yourself timed, as them guys don't look to linger too long in a place where they deliver money.

When the payroll is delivered, don't give them a chance to stick it in the safe, because then you'll only have to make them open the safe and you'll wind up shooting your way out. The best way is to time yourself, watch how many armored car men go up, and you watch for that same number to come down. When they are down, you bound right in and stick up the office help. Everybody knows just who to take. You wind up with the dough and screw out. In all cases you don't have to tie them up—just: "Throw them up!" jump into your car, and you get away.

Armored cars can be stuck up, in my opinion. If you get the drop on them, they go up like a kite. Two or three things you don't want to do—one is, to stick up an armored car. It's too risky. If I knew there was plenty of money in it, though, I'd take a chance. You would need four or five men.

Watch their deliveries, and when they get to a dead neighborhood, I would see how they open their doors. They always hold their hands on their guns. I know some tough guys that are in the underworld that carry a gun, and they wouldn't even shoot a cat. I know one thing, if you got a gun up to a man, he's going to respect you, because coppers and everyone respect it—as was just proven in a case right here in the City of New York at a Judge's dinner. I know of crap games where they got their guns taken off them, and got their heads kicked off in the bargain. Just don't give a damn'—step right up and take them.

So you got this armored car in a dead neighborhood. If they have soft tires, I would like to give them a slow puncture, but probably they would keep right on going until they get to their next delivery. That's a good idea, in giving them a flat, maybe they might get out and fix it. Sometimes you can forget yourself, no matter how smart you are; and when you forget for the moment a whole lot of things can happen.

They park in front of a factory. I would stick them up, wouldn't give them a chance to go in. I would stick up the first man and say: "Stick them up, you bastard!" and if they're going to shoot, I would let them shoot their own man. You hoist the three of them into their car and lock them in. You could get away with it. It's been done.

It's sometimes better to work where there's a crowd than where there's a dead neighborhood. Like snatching a payroll where a girl or fellow may be walking with a payroll right in the heart of Broadway. They think a guy won't stick them up because of the neighborhood. Some guys don't give a damn' where it is, because sometimes it's better to work where it's tougher than where it's easier. When a man goes out stealing, he don't go looking for a sure thing. He looks to make a sure thing out of it in order to avoid getting a pinch.

The best kind of a stickup in the long run is diamond guys, because if you get them, you're going to wind up with plenty of rubles.

The next best is payrolls and bookies on the racetrack. They are noted as shrewd articles. Not all of them are in the underworld. I would never look to stick up a man that is a regular guy.

There's some theatres you can stick up, where you can wind up with probably six grand. Then again, it's not really big money. You take the same risk for that as for $100,000, but you do that to keep yourself from going off the nut. It always pays to go out and steal big.

Another good case is when you stick up people with collat coming out of cabarets and some big night clubs. Here's a good way how to stick up what is known as society people, as they carry a lot of collat—what is known as jewelry. Go and park yourself up by a big opera house, say the Metropolitan, or any big place where there is going to be a big entertainment. Park yourself there and just watch out who is going in with the most stuff, or what stuff looks real good to you, as them people don't look to wear any phony stuff to them kind of affairs.

The next best move is to have a fellow dress up in a tux, and step right in back of them and be right behind them at all times. What I mean by that is, on their departure from the opera house they generally have a car waiting for them. They come with their own car. As you know, them people love to put on the ritz. One looks to show up with more stuff than the other, although I guess they're insured for it. When they look to step in their car, you have your car in position where it can pull right over to trail them.

You trail them, and if you can hoist them in a nice way in a dead street—I mean a good locality—cut their car off and send them in to the curb or the sidewalk. One or two men jumping out on the running board, one grabbing the chauffeur, sticking him up. Pull the guys out of the car and stop the motor. Then step inside and take them. You do everything as quick as possible. You take all the stuff she's got on her, yank it right off her throat, or look to take it right off her hands. Then screw away from there.

I know for a fact that there are guys, known as good flat thieves. A guy that's strictly out for jewelry and cash. They generally work on what is called funerals and funeral processions. Here's what I mean. Naturally, you know the man goes to work, probably even if he is a business man or a workingman, and if there's any children they probably go to school. Funerals are generally held after nine o'clock in the morning.

That lady, knowing that somebody died in her neighborhood, she's interested and looks out a window. These fellows snap a lock. Maybe she don't even lock the door. These fellows just know them locks anyway. To be truthful with you, I know a flat thief can work better while you are in the house than when you are out. Because when you are out he isn't going to get what he's looking for. While you're in, you're going to leave it in a drawer, or on top of the bureau or dresser.

I know a good flat thief's got plenty of money, because they are smart fellows. Here's how they work. Generally they work with a girl. In some cases they go out singly. They beat the flat themselves, alone. They have a girl downstairs. She's known as for the alibi. Like they're looking for rooms. It may be his wife, or a common law wife. Coney Island, in the summer time, is known as a good spot for flat thieves. They go down with the intention of hiring a room for the season.

They roam. Nobody sees their face, and if they do, the fellow has good connections as far as a bond is concerned, or as fixing. They wait for funerals, that's their main opportunity—funerals, or like parades. Anything to draw a woman to the window or to the door, or probably out into the street. Then they look to take jewelry and cash.

I won't say that they will look to hurt anybody, because I know that burglary in the first degree is committed after twelve midnight at the point of a gun or without a gun. If you enter a house after twelve midnight, you are going in there with the intent to kill. That's why they charge you with first degree burglary. Before that, it's second degree burglary. After twelve midnight you don't even need a gun.

You can make a buck with this water front racket—stealing freights. You use a motorboat to buy junk off steamships, tug-boats, or rope that they can't use no more. You might make a living out of that, but you're out to make more. You pull up alongside of a freight train that is being carried on the water as a freight boat—what is known as a car ferry. You might have a connection with the guy that has charge of that boat. You open up the freight car and put stuff on the motorboat, and bring it to your destination. You have about an hour and a half to work in. You look for the best train. You take a walk down the dock and see what train the good stuff is being heaved on, and get the number off the freight car. Silk, booze and stuff like that is the good stuff. Booze gets consigned to hospitals, etc. Or pull up to a freight yard and steal the freight out of the trains, and carry it down the dock and to the motorboat, drive off in your boat and bring it to your destination.

The loft racket is O.K. too. You can probably work with two trucks. You go and rent yourself a loft in a building probably next to it—next to the one you are going to clip—or probably in back of it. You will carry the stuff up to the roof and put it over to the roof where you have your loft, and take it down to your loft. If you are a smart fellow, take it to your loft. You can take it out in the daytime or that night. It is best to do it as quick as possible. But it is generally done in the morning to avoid suspicion.

Sometimes there is a loft where there is a million dollars' worth of silk and no other lofts around. You try to buy the cop on beat, and if he can't be bought, work while he is not there. You don't see him yourself; you try to make that connection. He doesn't know that you are going to do it.

A lofty works without a gun. The only one that has a gun is probably the outside man. They are not known as stickup guys. They are known as loft thieves. They are pretty clever, loft thieves. They just know what hour to bring the truck there. They work fast and get away. They break the lock, or get in through a window. If they happen to catch a watchman, they grab him and tie him up, and work while he is being tied up. It is a difficult job. You might catch him sleeping. Or you can say to them something, and they open up the door and you grab ahold of them, and if he hollers you push the door and tie him up. Before you pull a loft job, of course, you know whether there is a watchman or not. In the morning, when the people come that own the place, or the workers, they unloosen him and they tell him what happened.

As to pickpockets—when I was a kid I know hundreds of pickpockets. A good pickpocket is almost always a foreigner. They can open up your vest and get inside your vest. They can work on you without you knowing it. Take a case where there is a bus line. They work to get in with the chauffeur. The chauffeur is instructed what to do. He can tell if a cop is on the bus. The cop flashes his shield to him. A lot of cops get beat, too.

The persons are holding on to the straps. A guy gets in the front of the bus, which is jammed. He takes your pocket out gradually, and takes your money away from you. They can get into any pocket without you knowing it. If you catch them, they say it was a jam, and they say: "Pardon me."

Pickpockets rob each other, too. One will beat the other for his watch and chain, or for his money. If the other pickpocket happens to catch him, he says: "It is only a joke," but if he gets away with it, it is not a joke. They work in crowded places. They might work with a girl. They go to big social gatherings where there is large jewelry. They can take a necklace right off your neck, by clipping it on you. They get a couple of kids, give them boxing gloves, and start phony street fights. It starts a big gathering. The pickpockets are at work in the meantime. The kids get paid, but the pickpockets are at work beating girls for their week's pay, etc. They travel all over the country where they know there will be big doings, fights, etc. All leading cities send cops to said big cities, where there will be big gatherings, to inaugurations, etc. They wind up with money in the end, but they don't make money on a big scale. They work on a blind article, unless they are working on a tip. Sometimes they make good touches.

Chapter 8
MORE RACKETS

I know for a fact, any guy that goes into a cabaret with the intention of making a girl is out of his mind. Those girls are instructed only to sit with you and josh you along. Those girls are smartened up to that effect. They might make a date with you, and have you drink and drink and drink. When you are drunk, you'll get a check for probably three times as much. First of all, if a cabaret does serve liquor, they don't look to get you drunk too quick. You order a Scotch whiskey. That is cut with water under the faucet. They see that that don't get you drunk too quick. When they see that you are going, they give you bum booze—that is a racket. Another case is, if you pay off by a check, they raise your check.

I had twenty-five percent of a cabaret and had a big man come from Texas, and he was coming into the joint for two weeks straight. He was coming in because he fell in love with a little girl that was working as an entertainer. She was a good-looking kid, all right. In my opinion, I never went for looks in my life. As they say: "It is a good front, but nobody knows what is under." I was too smart for that. I never yet looked to make a cabaret girl or any hostesses. I knew I would not get the best of them.

She was too smart for him. She had him coming in all hours of the morning, spending $200 or $300 a night. She got a cut on that, twenty-five percent. Some of them, of course, just work on commission. But anyway, this man was a nice man. I was introduced to him. He said he was here to make a loan, for putting up electric lights in the said city that he came from. So I had a talk with him. I saw he was a regular man. If he bought me a drink I would buy him two. In that racket, if you do offer a boss a drink, you pay for both drinks. When a guy is going into them joints, he looks to make himself a big shot. But he is a sucker to the joint.

This man said to me: "I like that little girl, but I made a date with her yesterday and she didn't show up. I think I am going to another place." I used my head. He was in every night for two weeks straight, making big parties. I walked over to the girl and said: "Meet this guy once." I was looking out for my interest. I figured if she met him once she would not have to lay down for him. "Maybe he will buy you some clothes. I am not telling you to stay with him." I didn't care if that guy got laid or not. I wanted to see her meet him. She sat down and he made a date with her for the next day, and she did meet him. I guess he tried to steer her to a hotel, but he never came back to the joint any more. He was known to be a chump anyway, a sucker.

There are joints known as steering joints. It is more like a speakeasy, with a band in there. They work with what is known as cab drivers. They hand out cards. Sometimes a fellow comes in from out of town and says: "Say, maybe you can take us to a cabaret." Right away the driver steers him to this joint, and they are paid twenty-five percent of the bill. The man is drinking and drinking. They charge you seventy-five cents or $1 for each drink, and they raise your check anyway. If you drink $25 of liquor, you get a check probably for $40. You see, he has to take care of that cab driver, although the liquor only stands him probably $2 or $3. He is being taken again. They are known as chumps. He might offer one of the hostesses a drink and she will say to him: "What kind of liquor?" and will say: "That is too powerful," and "Oh, that is too strong." If she is not a good booster, the joint does not want her either. The joint probably gives her tea while the guy gets liquor.

Friends of mine came from out of town and I was looking to show them a good time. It was my motto to go to a cabaret. This night we went without any women. We could have made a couple of them hostesses at the cabaret. She made herself acquainted. I said to the hostess: "Get a couple of girls to keep us company." When I saw her order a bottle champagne, it hurt me, because I knew that if she would benefit out of it by having a good time she was only looking to make money for the joint; and I spilt the wine on her dress and paid for it.

I was not known as a chump in the cabarets, and I would not tell the hostess to sit down. If I wanted to dance, I would invite the girl to sit down. I don't carry my own liquor with me. If I stepped into a joint, I would look to spend a dollar. I never went to a cabaret and sat there drinking ginger ale. I could get that in an ice cream soda. If I did step into a joint, I always showed myself regular. I always bought my liquor there. In a joint like the —— —— Club, I know they will charge me too much money, and in them kind of places they only look for the cover charge. If a fellow is known as a good fellow they will not put a cover charge on. In them kind of joints, if I thought I could get liquor there and it was good liquor, I would buy it there. But if I thought it was not good liquor, I would bring my own, knowing that it was good.

There are people—and the banks know it—that can cash a check and put it over on leading banks, and, can duplicate a man's handwriting. How do they do it? They pick on a guy that has a lot of dough, that carries a big checking account. They get one of his blanks and one of his canceled checks. The fellow that gets those things gets twenty-five percent if the deal goes over. The only way he can get that is either through a friend of his, or he may be a friend of yours. The bank is always stuck. He says: "Hello, Jack, I want you to make me out a check for $5 or so. I want to pay my electric bill. Here is $5. Give me a check."

They have your handwriting. They don't look to cash that check. They want that check to know how you sign the check. The next move they do, is try to get one of your blanks. They stay around in your office and see where you keep your check book. Of course, you can't go into a bank and say: "So and so sent me down for a book of blank checks." If they don't know you, they will want the signature of that man. But you might get it. Anyway, he might have a name on his check, as: "John Henry Jones, Clothing Manufacturer," or "Real Estate Broker," printed right on the check, which the bank looks to accommodate the depositors in that way. Real estate men are best, because they carry big checking accounts, and banks know that they always do business on a big scale and have to cash big checks.

The next move they make is, they get that check. Probably the fellow that is getting the checks might never see the forger. He is working through another source that is in with the forger. The blank check is then delivered and, to tell the truth, there are guys that can duplicate your own handwriting better than you can yourself. The next move, you open up a bank account. You bring a kid along with you, and you instruct them: "This here is my messenger from my place of business. Any time there is money deposited it will be through him." The next move, you don't make any more deposits, as far as putting up cash. The next deposit you make is with a check. You send a $10,000 or $15,000 check to the said bank with the party that you recommended to the bank that will make the deposits and withdrawals. That is placed on your account. They work on three days' time. They know it has to go through the Clearing House, and they ring up the bank and find out how much they got in their account. Right here and there you know that everything is on the up and up. You send up that party to make the withdrawal, and they take that money out.

Later on, the bank puts it on the statement of the party. He knows that he never issued that kind of a check to this party, and probably don't know the name that is on the check. Of course you always make a deposit and open an account in a phony name. He goes down to the bank—the party whose name has been forged—and makes a holler. His bank makes an investigation. They compare handwritings and see that it ain't his handwriting. There is a loophole right then and there. They argue it out. Anyway, the depositor is always in the front. The bank does not want to lose him as a depositor. They are looking to accommodate everybody as far as holding their depositors. The bank notifies the Burns Detective Agency about it. They look and look for the forger. I know one thing, they always catch the punk. They never get the main guy.

They also pass phony checks in crap games. Some guys lose so much money they get desperate. They have a friend of theirs make out a check, and he goes to the crap game and cashes the check. They look to accommodate him and they give him the cash, and he plays and wins and walks out. Three or four days later they find out it is a phony check. They look for this guy for their money back. If they catch him, he says: "I will see if I can see this guy and get the money back." He tells them to redeposit the check. They generally try to find out as to whether there is a depositor by that name.

There are all kinds of means to get a check cashed. You go to a cabaret, go there three or four times. The fellow sees you there and that you are a pretty fair customer. You go in there with a party and you pay with a check. You can go into a haberdashery in your own neighborhood. They want to accommodate you, and cash your check. It is cheap stuff, but it is forgery. Some guys go out and steal and steal, and the party that is buying the stuff pays off with a check.

As to counterfeiting, I don't know how they make the plates. They get the paper from Canada. I don't know just where. They go to a dead neighborhood and they work—print it—at nights when people are sleeping. Then they are sold 35 for $100.

There are different ways you pass the money. You might make some married woman. She has a lot of jewelry. You tell her you know a guy that will buy it. You have a guy set up with this phony money. You bring her to him and pay her off. She don't know it is phony money. When she goes to change that money they find out that it is phony money. She might say I gave her $5,000 for $8,000 of jewelry. The bank notifies her that it is counterfeit money. They pinch her. They find out that she has just been duped out of her jewelry, and that she has been stuck with that money. That money is useless to her.

Or, you go and eat in a restaurant and pay the cashier off, and when the cashier tries to cash it he finds out that he is stuck.

Another good way is to go and make yourselves that you want to buy a lot of booze, and you can pay off a guy like that. On the water, where big ships come in, they step up and pay the captain off with phony dough. He don't know nothing, but they find out a little later. They go all over the country and cash them. They go anywhere, to France.

Any guy that got sense don't carry more than one on his person. When you want to cash a lot, you have to carry more than one. You are taking it on a sure thing. You know that there are no cops around and no Federal people trailing you. Maybe the party that you are going to cash it does not even know that you are going in to cash it. Where small business people are—candy stores, cigar stores—you just carry one on your person, have it mixed up with good money. When you have cashed that one, you go back and get another one. You can get rid of probably $1,000 worth in a half hour. Even banks get stuck with that money. They get put in by their own depositors. When it comes to a final checkup, they see that they got stuck with probably a $20 or $50 bill in their hands. They are insured for that, anyway. They at once notify the Federal Government and they send down officials.

There are a lot of sources you can get it from. I get it from the main source. I don't know where they get it from. I am not interested. I don't care who makes it or don't make it. I am just interested in getting it.

Dope—that's the best racket in the world, but I don't know nothing about it.

I never smoked any of that stuff. I seen plenty of it smoked, but I hate them guys. I got some good friends that are smokeys. I used to lay pipey broads. I know four schoolteachers that are smoking with a little friend of mine for the last two years. Every afternoon, about ten after three, they come up to his apartment—come with their own stuff, and lay down and smoke—and they just want to get laid, too. A Chink is known as the best lover, I had a broad once tell me.

I once met a broad and she wanted me to smoke a pipe. I brought myself up a corncob pipe with Ivanhoe tobacco and said this would charge me up. She wanted me to take dope. Some pipeys says it's as good as drinking booze. I said: "I'll drink the booze."

A smokey never drinks, because it will hurt him. You can't drink and use drugs, because you will wind up in the graveyard. I can show you guys that smoke for twenty hours out of the twenty-four. One thing I can say, a fellow that smokes a pipe will always wind up a snowey. You have to smoke that stuff indoors, and it is smoked with wet towels on the doors and windows.

There are a lot of people like to smell that stuff. They wouldn't smoke it. They will go and buy stuff, and go down to the East Side and lay around, just to smell them fumes. It's got a sweet odor, but it makes me sick.

I used to get a kick out of them pipeys—go up and knock on the door. They think it's cops, and they will throw the pipes and everything else out of the window.

It gives you a sensation to know what you are doing. The pipey is always keen when he is fooling with that stuff. He's a shrewd fellow. He's shrewder when smoking that stuff than you or I are now, and it makes them do things that they don't want to do themselves.

There's more junk around than opium. They say smoking a pipe is just a pleasure. They call themselves pleasure smokers. It develops into a habit, you get known to be a hospitable pipey. The next thing you know, you may be in a theatre or some place, and seeing that you can't get away, and say: "If I only had a smoke I would feel better." Then they take morphine. Once a guy starts into coke, it will eat his brain away. They usually take morphine or heroin.

To my opinion, it would make me sick. I don't say you can't get a kick out of anything that will make you sick. They say it makes them feel good. I don't know. But I see the after-effects—they can't eat and they can't do anything. Did you ever see a pipey after smoking four or five months? He's all pale and run down from smoking that stuff.

Hasheesh—that's the name of the hop. There's all grades, just like coffee. There's yensheesh, hasheesh, and the brick is the most expensive and the best. The other stuff comes in liquid form, like grease. That's how they smoke it. You take a piece of the stuff and roll it around, and take and heat it up at a lamp. Heat it up until it gets hard, just like cement would. Then they put it on this little stove, what they call a lamp, and they just mix it around until it gets hard. When hard, they make a little ball out of it, and put it into the hole of the pipe, and draw and smoke. They can't stop it when they once get in it.

I have done thirty days and I have seen junkeys in all my times in prison, and they say: "When I get out I'll never use it." Promise his head off, and say: "I won't do it no more." The next thing you know he's doing it again. It's just like smoking a cigarette, in fact it's worse than a cigarette—you don't have to use a holder, either, to stay away from it. They give them cures and cures, but it don't do them no good. Ninety percent of them break in through a broad. They want to show themselves wise guys. In my opinion they are God damn' dopes, going up smoking a pipe with a broad. The broad is more dope than they are. She wants to get a kick out of it. He thinks it's an honor if he smokes a pipe. But the only honor it is, he's doing himself injustice. So far as his health is concerned, he is ruining himself.

Chapter 9
HOW TO RUN A CRAP GAME

A whole mob can't get a crap game to go. It's always got to be one fellow that's very well liked by cops and the underworld, and by all other sorts of people—business men, and so forth. Naturally, to run a crap game you got to be a good fellow. What I mean is, a guy that any guys would follow. I know, myself, I would gamble on a graveyard. Not only I but a thousand others. There's a lot of guys that's known as chiselers in crap games. They can probably step in with ten dollars.

A guy that steps in with ten or fifty or a hundred dollars is out of his kind, because in a thing like that a guy is depending on luck. There's no guy living can say he can take you in that manner. The only guy I consider a wise guy in a crap game is the book, and then sometimes he gets taken. A smart gambler never plays to a book, it's only the chump.

I know if I had a thousand dollars in my hand, I would look for to gamble with a guy that's got two thousand. When I clip him, I would walk away and look for another guy that's got more than me.

There's a thing what is known as luck in that racket. Although sometimes the dice are ice cold all night, and sometimes they may be red hot. I know one thing, that a guy with plenty of money should never play right—I mean, to bet with the point. What is known in a crap game as right and left—with the dice and against the dice.

To my opinion, the dice are dummies and the only way I would gamble is when they are hit up against the boards. Although there are guys that is known to use crooked dice. But not in a real, standard crap game, because a standard crap game isn't going to let anybody cheat the player. All crap games are run without arguments—everybody has got to be a gentleman there. I wouldn't shoot crap with red dice. No particular reason—just because.

You can start a crap game with five hundred dollars or two hundred. But if you want to start a crap game on a bigger scale, you got to work with a combination. You got to declare people in.

Sometimes you take people in on their reputation, because that saves the game sometimes from a stickup; and when people knows that so and so is in on the game they will go and gamble.

Generally if a guy looks to declare himself in, that way, he is known as a bulldozer. If you are going to declare anyone in on your game, you ain't going to have no respect for him in your heart, knowing that in case of loss you are going to be the one stuck, he ain't going to lose nothing, where I got to stand there, maybe, and book a game for four or five hours a night.

The next best move, I would go around in the neighborhood where there is crap games being run, and where I know there is money fellows. I don't mean fellows that's got millions. I mean fellows like in the newspaper racket, as far as the delivery guys is concerned. They got gambling in their hearts, because I know in my heart they are either all former racket guys, and they can't get along on that salary that they get as a newspaper man.

With five thousand I wouldn't be a damn' fool. I would say to myself: "No use losing the five thousand in a night." Although in a chiseling crap game you can't lose it. Because, what is known, the guy that's got more capital than the other always takes the guy that's got less. But when you only got one thousand, you shoot with a guy that's got two thousand.

You make up a rule that they can't get more than two hundred on a ten and two hundred on a four, and that you won't lay more than one-fifty odds against a hundred on five and nine and on six and eight, which to a book is like what is known as cream. You lay six to five on such a bet. You always limit your play. The biggest crap games in the country are limited, because a smart gambler don't stay in too long. If he's a left player, he catches a couple of misses and if he's a right player he takes a couple of points, and walks away.

There is another thing, that is known as guys that shoot crap for just their expenses—their expenses of the day. Some guys say: "I got fifty bills, and all I want to make is fifteen or twenty dollars." I have seen guys that already tried to do that kind of stuff, and have seen them lose thousands, because they would never limit themselves; and if they do limit themselves they get taken, too.

You ain't no smart player when you back up a thousand dollars to win fifteen or twenty.

If you are going into a crap game with a thousand dollars you should stand to win at least double your money, and walk away. You ain't compelled to stay there if you don't want to. People think: "Don't you get killed if you are going to walk away from that game?" If you are stuck he ain't going to give you back your money!

I know guys that are known as sure thing guys as far as gambling is concerned, and they ain't got a damn' nickel, although they can lay their hands on money.

You hold this crap game in the newspaper building, say, and you stake a watchman or so. Or you shoot crap on the street and stake the cops a couple of bucks not to bother you, and they'll notify you in case any bulls are coming. You give up a few bucks, knowing that you are always going to make them few bucks. Then the crap game is established.

It's already established between themselves. They're already shooting crap there. You go up and join in. You can be known as a book. You pull a connection through a fellow that's probably running the crap game. What I mean, he probably cuts the game so much on every pass.

Another way how to go and book games. There's a lot of crap games being held by them cloak and suit manufacturers. They have games between themselves. They always have what is known as protection. They always let in somebody because, as you know, in that racket, the cloak and suit racket, or probably any other place where there is unions concerned, the boss always tries to keep connection with the underworld, figuring in case of trouble he can have some people to be with him.

He may say some day he's going to shoot crap, and you say: "I'm going to declare myself in," which anybody that is in this racket tries to do. Although there are a lot of fellows that don't care for them kind of rackets, because them kind of rackets wind up in jealousy and committing murder.

You go up one day and act as a gentleman. The second time up you are a gentleman. Naturally, one day, probably, you have a guy there cutting the game. Then you declare yourself in.

The next best move to make is to try to get a book in there, because the book will probably give you from fifteen to twenty-five percent for said information as to where to book a game. He steps in and is in the middle. He'll take bets right or left or any way. If you want to bet right or left—say you want to bet fifty he loses. He bets you he don't lose. Another bets fifty he don't lose, and he takes the bet. He collects five dollars. When you bet right, the book always takes your money. When you bet left, the book always collects one way. Any fellow who knows anything won't play where the book plays both ways. It's bad enough the book takes you one way without taking you both ways. That's worse than sticking you up.

I might know a fellow that's working down a newspaper racket, and he may tell me: "Danny, I know a sweet game—I always shoot crap in a certain place." Naturally, I ask him to take me in, and I produce a big bankroll. All gamblers try to creep in and get that dough. One fellow says: "Go ahead, you want to book the game?" I say: "Sure, why not?" Then you get to be known as the book. If there is anybody cutting the game, you give him a percent for giving you that information and letting you book there.

The book is always going to play square. Every time you go to a crap game, before the game starts you take a count of the money that he is going to go in with, and at the end of the play you take another count, and if there is any losses or winnings, you mark them down. At the end of the month you tally up, and if there is any winnings you split.

I don't say everybody could run a crap game. Don't think you can go around and conquer the world overnight.

You start a crap game like this newspaper office. That game gets going. You get a good booky in there, and you get a fifteen percent cut. You know you can trust him.

Then you start a game going in a clothing house, say. You can have the same booky booking that. He gives a friend of his enough money, and he is known he is handling the money for such a book. He pays that fellow probably a salary, or a percent of the play. You still get your fifteen percent.

A crap game can last until the cops—what I mean, not the cops on beat or probably station house cops, but what is known as Inspector's men from headquarters—break it up. They generally work on a tip. They all work on information. They find out there's a game running at such a place, and they try to get in. They get the information through a player.

Maybe that player may tell friends of his that ain't a player there, and that's how information is given out. Probably a fellow may be married and tell his wife, and his wife, seeing him come home without any money, will make a holler.

I had a place on the lower East Side and I had a mob of fellows coming in there, some of them married men. They used to stay all night and gamble, playing cards and shooting crap. Some weeks they would win and their wives would be happy, and if they lost they would blame it on me. She one time gave information to the cops that I must be running a whore-house. She says: "He is running crap games, and must have girls in there." I never made money through women.

That's a standard crap game. You got to work that through politicians. You have to be broad-minded enough. In order to make a buck, you got to give a buck. What I mean, if you are going to make it, you got to spend it. So you go and make yourself connection with the leader of your district. Well, as you know, everything is political all over the country. Every district carries a captain. Probably you do a lot of work for that captain on election. Any fellow that's got sense as far as racketeering, or where he knows he is out stealing, that he's got to go for a favor to them said people. He don't look to make any money off them politicians. What I mean by that is, he won't kill nobody, but will look to do as he is told by the political captain.

Naturally, you know if you work at an election, and if your vote is bought—what I mean, bought, is where the politician gives up say two or five or ten dollars for a vote—that is marked down on the book, and you are like blackballed if you ever go for a favor.

Naturally, the fellow that's going to run a crap game, he makes himself a connection with the captain, with that understanding that if everything turns out all right he expects a favor, too—as to opening of a crap game. Although you can run a crap game without cops knowing it; but when they do know, they're going to raid it and the game is all over, unless you keep running all over the neighborhood.

The only way I would run a game, look to keep myself in solid with the leading politician of the district. Do him a favor, and don't take no money in exchange for the favor; but when I would come for a favor he can't afford to turn me down, and if he would turn me down I would go against him, because I'm looking for only one thing, and when I get that I will do anything for that one thing.

Naturally, I start the game. I would tell him: "Listen, so and so, I'm going to open a crap game and don't want to be bothered by any cops." Naturally, if you do get bothered, get pinched, some Judge will hear the case, and nine times out of ten all games like that are discharged by the magistrates, and sometimes the Judge tells the cops: "Why don't you go out and get stickups?" Or sometimes you get yourself a mouthpiece for $25, and a Judge, seeing him, discharges the case, just seeing his face. Or else a politician phones the Judge and the case is discharged.

As I said before, you got to give up a buck to make a buck. Don't think you can run without giving up. First of all, you got to see every cop that's on the beat where the crap game is being held. You got to go and see if you can do business with the precinct captain. Maybe he won't take money or booze. Then you make him a present on his birthday, or like if they come for the loan of money, you can't afford to turn him down. If you don't get that back, you say: "Stuck!" That always comes out of the book's money.

The fellow that's running the game, he's the main guy. He don't do anything. He just looks in once or twice a week, or maybe every night, and walks out. Then there's the booky. He's got to pay the protection in the crap game, so much a night. That is known as the expense. Before the booky starts in to book his crap game, everything is counted up as to what he is going to open up for in that game. They might open up with one bankroll, and the game might go for three bankrolls. Everything is accounted for.

The first thing he does, is take off the expenses for the help and the protection. If it's a good size crap game, there's a good fifteen fellows protecting it, inside and outside. Probably a hundred fellows are playing. I seen crap games pinched with 280 fellows in the game. With five sets of dice. After they hit the board, the dice man grabs them and shakes them. Just one guy is shooting dice at a time. There are two tables running. Maybe 150 betting at one table and 100 at the other table. They all bet.

All the bets don't go through the booky. If I can lay you six to five, why should I lay him six and a quarter to five? The only thing I pay for is when the dice comes around to me. He says: "Are you picking them up?" I say: "No, I'm passing," and throw him a quarter. The guy that says he can knock off five passes, I think is off his head.

There may be a good fellow that's got a good mob, and he may be declared in for a night's pay, for protection. Say, like I'm a good friend of yours, and I'm running a crap game. I know I can't push you in that crap game, to say you are in. For this reason, when you open a crap game, there's a lot of guys looking to get jobs in the crap game.

To my estimation, any guy that works in a crap game is a guy that won't go out and steal, and is looking for an easy dollar. To my opinion it ain't any crime to work; but they can't work, so they chisel around until they get in on a crap game.

You can't push everybody in there. Say I'm a good friend to you and I'm running a crap game. I say: "I can't push you in there because it's going to look too lousy." I say: "I'll give you ten percent of my cut." If he's a friend for money, he's no good. Some say: "My friend is the buck that's in my pocket." Them guys wind up when they get pinched and they look for friends to go to help them. People remember what he said—the buck is his friend. To hell with him. Why should I give him a buck?

Why should I declare him in? The guy that's out to make a dollar on his own friend is no good. If I seen that I was friends with a fellow, and he can't be a friend to me without looking to make a buck through me, I would shim that guy.

I can't declare you in on this game, but I will see you anyway, even if I got to buy you a suit of clothes. Anybody that's running a crap game is known as a reliable fellow that way. What I mean is, if a fellow that he don't even know, a player, says: "Gees, I just went broke and I got to pay my rent tomorrow!" Maybe he don't lose that much, or maybe he won. But you got to fix him up. You got to be known as a good fellow.

A punk can't run those games, because when people get to know he's a punk, they'll push him right out, and if he's going to look for trouble he'll get plenty. His friends even turn against him and say: "He's only out for himself. We'll go with this here mob; we can make money with this mob."

You pay the dice man a salary. Say, ten bucks a night. Say I am the booky. No more than I step in, I count out my dough what I got. Then I figure out how much men is working in the game, and I hand out that expense before I start to gamble. Everything is marked down, and at the end of the night I always got to have what I opened up with. I count off as to what I first came into the game with. After that, if there is any winnings, over and above the said money what I produced before the time of the game, and expense as to cops and people working in the game, that is all marked down, and if any losses, that is marked down too. Although, say I open up with five thousand and my expenses, maybe, for the night, is $120. Say I lose $100 for the night. That would be like part of the expenses, although that is the loss of the game.

The crap game don't start until after twelve at night. The book gets together with the fellow that's interested in the game, and they go and talk it over, and they figure up, and whoever interested in the game is with them in another room. Why should everybody be there in the one room where business is being held?

Only those that put up for an interest in the game are in on this. Say, like a game with a five thousand bankroll. If you went ten percent of that game, you have to put up $500 for ten percent. You put up $500. If the book gets stuck $500 that night, you would have probably $50 taken off your $500. Where if it's a case where he loses the whole $5,000, and if I ain't got more money to produce in the morning to him, I am out, as far as the game is concerned. I always got to have money to produce for the next play, but it's rarely a case like that, where you got to produce that said money. Because it always calls for the book to take that kind of game.

The guys that is playing with the books are supposed to be a chump. But at the end they go to the crap game and shoot and shoot and lose thousands of dollars, so everybody winds up what is known as behind the eight ball. I don't know why they call it that.

Chapter 10
TAKING A CRAP GAME

I would never look to stick up a man, myself, what is known as a regular fellow, and another thing, I would never look to stick up a crap game, because I shoot crap myself and it's only a punk that looks to stick up them kind of games.

There is crap games among big business men. Them kind of guys, all right. They gamble a whole lot between themselves. Naturally, somebody finds out about it, which is noted. No matter how much you look to keep a secret, you will confide in somebody to tell it to.

Maybe you might get information this way: A fellow might be working in a place of business, and his boss might say to him: "Gees! I lost five thousand dollars last night." Naturally, he thinks he's boasting, but with his boasting he might be sometimes giving a good bit of information to a fellow. That's just the way you get your information. Usually them guys that boast to look to make themselves a wise guy, wind up being taken. Them are the guys that are easy to take, them what is called legitimate business men.

Here's how to work it. When you get the information that big business men have a private game in such a spot, you watch it for one or two times being played. You try to enter the building where they are playing. Maybe they are playing in a club. Naturally, they will have a doorman, and that doorman just knows who's who. There's only one thing to do. When you see players going in and going out, you watch the ones that is going in and you pick yourself a guy, and two men step up to him and put rods right into his side and tell him: "Keep your mouth shut, we want to get in." Naturally, he is scared, and you push him right in with you, the doorman thinking he is coming with a couple of friends. When you get inside you take the doorman, and when you get inside to the crap game, you stick them all up.

I might be walking the street some time and they will say: "There's one of the guys that stuck up the game." Naturally, it leads to a lot of trouble. That's how the murders are committed, because they have guys on their payroll and look to see who you are. They might come up to you in a nice way and ask for the dough back. You are going to deny it, and it winds up in a shooting match.

One thing I can say, I never yet gave up a nickel to a cop as far as running a crap game. I have had twelve cops bust in on me, and detectives come to me from Police Headquarters and said: "If this place ain't closed in forty-eight hours—" I said: "To hell with you, this is a legitimate place, an automobile renting place."

A cop came over to me and said: "What have you got, a game in there?" He was looking to get seen. I wasn't making enough money to see them. The first thing you know, you would see the whole station house, and then maybe they would pinch you.

I don't say it's a crap game where you can win millions, but I do say the lowest that was won at the end of a month was $19,240, and that was to be split up by the fellows interested in the crap game, with expenses all paid out. Expenses amounted to something like $500 to one squad, what is known as an Inspector's Squad; and $500 to another squad. The Inspector's men travel four or five in a squad. You figure a sawbuck a night to probably the captain of the said station house, and then maybe two bucks a night to the cop on beat, and maybe a cop may come off another beat. You know he's a good fellow, but he's just taking advantage for that lousy two bucks, and he creeps in. You give up to one and you're going to have twenty on you to give them dough, too.

They know the game is running, and so many complaints being sent in about that game, they have to send someone around to the head of the game and show him the letters, and say: "We are going to get in trouble." The fellow at the head of the game says: "O.K., I'll give you a pinch." He gives them a phony pinch—what I mean, he gets a mob of fellows that ain't any racket guys, that are probably out of work. They are just punks that seek a reputation. They would lay in the can all night and think it's an honor to be called up before the Judge for a crap game.

He gets a lot of fellows and they go and engage an apartment in that vicinity, like a cellar. They give a housekeeper five dollars to use a cellar, or if there are empty rooms, they use them. Then the police crash in and say: "Stick them up, you sons of bitches!

Line up, there!" Although it's a real pinch, but you are going to get discharged.

The cops step in and make it look real. They pinch everybody, take them to the station house and book them, and that covers them for another month.

All these punks get taken to the station house and booked. They get bailed right out and appear the next morning before a Judge, and he hears the case. If there's any fine, the book is always there, or the fellow at the head of the game, to pay the fine. The real crap game, in the meantime, is going on just the same. It don't go on during the pinch, because it would look lousy, and that you are taking advantage of the cops.

Maybe a month later they get a lot more complaints. The Inspector says: "You got to get that crap game!" Probably the Inspector will come himself, which I know that an Inspector walked up to a crap game. He heard a noise in a loft building. He went downstairs and says to the cop on beat: "Is there any crap game running around here?" He says: "No, not that I know of." This Inspector was one of the toughest Inspectors in the Police Department. He says: "If that crap game ain't pinched, I want to see you in the morning and, furthermore, there's a crap game in such a building and I want you to go up there and lead these men in." The Inspector knew that cop was getting a couple of bucks. He had to take them on account of political influence. You got to do them cops a favor.

The Inspector led the raid himself, and he pinched the crap game, catching a couple of guns, although nobody admitted to owning the guns, although they don't look to make too much of investigation of a crap game that's got guns, because they know the guns are there for protection. If a player gets stuck up, he ain't going back there again.

One night a couple of bulls broke in a crap game where I had an interest. I happened to have a —— on my person, and there was a fellow at the door. A crap game has a password. There's a man outside, probably a few blocks away. A crap game isn't being held in one spot all the time. You can gamble in one place for a month and then go back again. Maybe move to and fro, but you don't have to keep moving out of the vicinity, because a player will travel from here to hell for a crap game. This outside man directs them.

A fellow was coming up the stairs, and when this bull seen him, he put a gun in his side and said: "Give me the password." He said: "Who the hell are you?" He figured it was a stickup and he wouldn't give the information, fearing that he would get killed and get implicated in the crime of robbery. He got kicked down the stairs, and the bull knocked on the door and gave another password to the doorman. The doorman forgot himself and opened the door, and let him in. I steps out with a —— in my hand. He hit me on the chin with the butt of his gun and knocked me nearly cold. I heard him say: "Don't worry, boys, I'm just an officer of the law." Later I got up and he says: "Get over there, you," and I happened to stand near a barrel. They made a search and they found two guns underneath where the book was playing. When they found several guns, they searched every player, thinking they might find a gun on them. If a fellow gets found with a gun on him, the fellow running the crap game will always look to do business, as to save that fellow from a pinch, and if it can't be done he will look to bail him out and help him in other ways, to help him out.

A gun was found in the barrel. He said: "Who owns that gun?" Nobody answered. He says to me: "Is that your gun?" I wouldn't admit it was. I said: "No, it ain't my gun." Anyway they made a pinch of me, and they booked me in the station house. He swore blue Christ that I had a gun in my hand looking to stick him up. I thought he was a stickup guy, but I wouldn't shoot a guy looking to stick up a crap game. I would look to get him in another way. So I always use my head about them there punks and, to tell you the truth, I never yet carried a gun then or now in no crap game. They couldn't give me enough money to carry a gun. I know if I get caught with a gun, it's going to cost me plenty of money, or I would get plenty of time.

Still and all, I could get any kind of a city job, except a cop's job. A man can be wanted for a stickup when he comes out of Elmira, and they won't touch him. Why? Because the Elmira Reformatory is noted for a place where they reform criminals; but to my opinion nobody is reformed in them places, because you mingle with them people who tell you how to learn more.

In them reformatories there is always a Board of Parole. I know the President of the Board of Parole. He is one of the leading lawyers of the day. He's a man by the name of Henry Melville. I got two years' parole once. I never worked a day since I was out, and I only done one year parole out of the two years.

I don't say everything is done with money. You got to use political influence too, because if you offer money they are going to turn on you.

I seen myself protecting a game one night on the outside, with a doorman. He was a pipey. While standing with him, a car happened to pull up. Them kinds of squads pull up with Ford touring cars. Out stepped four bulls. It was in the winter time, and we had a fire going in a milk can with the head of the can cut off.

I was supposed to stand a little way from him, figuring that if stickup guys would come, they might get away with the money but they would never get away with the stickup. We would either get the money back and don't have trouble, or else don't get the money back and have plenty of trouble.

This night the bulls stepped up, and these bulls happened to be on the payroll getting $500 a month. The crap game happened to be running in the back of a big candy store. They stepped up and says to this fellow: "What are you doing here?" I says: "I'm waiting for my partner to come down, to go to work down the fruit market." He knew the doorman, and says: "Where's the game?" They says to me: "Where's that crap game, you, or we'll put your head in that fire." I said: "I'm no gambler and I don't know of any crap game."

I had a —— on my person, and it was on my mind maybe they'll give me a frisk. I know I wouldn't let a cop pinch me with a gun; I would clip him first. I ain't making any money with the gun, why should I carry it and get pinched with it? That would hurt me, to do a bit for a lousy gun, where I know in other cities you don't get a day for a gun, whereas in this city a fellow with a record, like me, might get seven or fourteen years.

I just used my head and answered their questions, which is always my motto: "Be nice and use your head." Seeing they couldn't get no information out of me, they says: "That game is run in this here building." They ran into a different building.

In I ran and says to the fellow that was left in charge, known as the cutter—the fellow that throws the dice to the player, and he collects. Every crap game is run this way—a quarter if you pass and a half dollar if you pick up the dice. I said: "Everybody be quiet, there's a law out there. Put out the light and be quiet and we'll sneak out after a while."

After notifying them, the game stopped. The bulls came out and says: "There's no game in there." I had the —— gone, so they hit me a smack on the chin. I knew it calls for it, so I took it. They do that to show you how tough they are. They came out and we were still standing by the fire. They didn't know that I had notified the crap game, but later on the fellow that was left in charge, seeing the cops didn't come, says: "What the hell did you run in for? Look how much we are losing now." Naturally, I told the main feller that was running the game I would like to kill that son of a bitch that he left in charge. He happened to be a brother-in-law of his. I never liked that bastard in my heart, but through his brother-in-law's good name he was making a buck. One night we took confidence in him and let him book the game, and he ran away with the money. I never seen him to this day.

There's other ways of taking in gambling. You set up dice with quicksilver. There's other crap games run that are illegitimate. What I mean, where they think a game is going to be a standard game and probably where there's a lot of money.

They call it a sucker's game. One guy starts the game, and gets him a book who gets about twenty or twenty-five percent of the game. That kind of book is known as a cheater. He says: "These guys are mugs, they don't know nothing about shooting crap." Somebody says: "Why don't you get new dice?" They say: "Them lousy dice are hard luck." Here's how you work that.

You get yourself about a hundred pairs of dice. What I mean, pairs is not twos, but sets. There's five in a set. Any guy that knows anything about this, the right size of dice is five-eighths of an inch. Most books carry the rule with them to measure the dice and square them off.

You make yourself a connection with a candy store near your place, where they sell dice, and you walk in and hang around and act like a good customer. You talk to him and you know they always buy the dice in that place. Maybe they buy in another place. It's a good practice to go to all places where they buy the dice. You say: "Hello, Mr. Rovinsky." You know he's working on a small margin of profit. You say to him: "Listen, Mr. R., I'm going to leave some dice here, and if anybody should come to call for dice, you sell them these dice, and I'll pay you good for every set that you sell."

Them dice is generally bought by a book himself for $5 a set in a standard crap game, but not that kind of a crap game he don't pay that, because in a crap game you need at least three sets of dice and why should a chiseler's crap game go to the expense of $5 a set for dice? The $5 dice is guaranteed, with your initial on—"J" for Jack. In case a dice goes off the table, that dice that gets thrown off the table is picked up by the dice man and handed to the book, who looks for the initial, and if that dice has been chipped, he throws it aside.

Anyway, them dice is set up in all the candy stores in the vicinity. You have them dice circulated, and when you go into the game you will know they're your dice. A player says: "Here's five bucks. Go out and get me a set of dice."

You already got it made up with the man in the store that every pair of dice that is sold, you will either give him a buck or two bucks. They think they're getting the dice legitimate. They come up and get taken.

The book is this way. A fellow that's a booky always has got to have his head. What's the good of a guy booking a game if he can't use his head? The book is like a bank, he's got plenty of money. He takes it or lays it.

Why should I let you in there with my money, when you don't know how to handle it? Sometimes you have bets this way—I am laying you $150 on a said point—on a five or a nine. If the man misses and don't make the point, that's left, that $150 is yours. If he makes the point, you got to give him a hundred of your money, which is $255, and if it's right, its $150 and that $5 you take. A man that's in the box to be a book is known as a fellow with a good head. He might have five bets left, and there may be a lot of money on that way. He's going to look for a right play to edge that play off, so as to cover himself so he wouldn't be betting out his money, and will collect the "vigorish." The book just knows how dice are going, right or left, although dice are dummies, but what is known in a crap game as hot or cold. That's the first question a gambler asks entering a crap game, whether it's going hot or cold.

Some guys get a habit of playing the way the dice are going. This here book just knows how to bet with these dice that he's already had set up. They may be known as left dice or right dice.

Say his plan is right, and right away he's going to look to edge himself off, one way or the other. If the plays is left, he is going to look for all the left bets he can get.

Another thing, I know that the books of crap games, they carry what is known as book dice. What I mean by book dice is, that they won last month with these dice. Every night they buy new dice.

I was interested in the game. I was never a dice man. That's work, being in that box, hollering out numbers. You can get a sore throat. I knew when the dice was in. The book figures on them, dice that they're already worn down, and they have that hunch, that feeling, what is known to a gambler.

I know, myself, I was interested in a certain game in Brooklyn. At this particular game a player happened to get taken. He was looking to take other people, and couldn't stand to be taken himself. He happened to lose and the book happened to win—although the book didn't win his money. This player, believing he knows about dice, said that they had phony dice in the game. I heard about it and went over to this guy. I said: "Listen, you punk," and I took an axe and I said: "I'll give you all of these dice and if you can prove to me that they're phony, I'll give back every cent in the game. But if they're not, I'll take your God damn' head off." I didn't happen to be the book, but I happened to be interested. I was just burned up so much against him. It hurt me to see that kind of a bum make a holler. I wouldn't mind if a legitimate person made a holler. I would say: "What are you hollering about? Here's the dice. You mustn't talk that way. That's going to hurt the game." When a crap game is run, it's run on the level. The book is just got that hunch that he can win with these dice. They're straight dice and aren't fixed up.

Suppose we came in to shoot crap, but if I think they are putting anything over on me, I'll look to pick up one anyway and look it over. I see how the edges are worn down or if there's quicksilver inside. If so, I'll say: "I don't want to play." I'll say: "What do you want, my money without a gun? Here, take it."

Chapter 11
HOW ONE THIEF BEATS ANOTHER

They say there's honor among thieves. There's honor, all right, while you are making money, but don't trust them too much. What I mean by trusting is, don't leave your money around any place where he can pick it up, because it's born in him, and what's born in him he will take anything that ain't nailed down. I know, because I have seen it worked in prisons, where they would even steal your toothpaste and even change your pillow cases on you—take a clean one for a dirty one. They don't care how they hurt you, so long as they feel good.

Here's a case. Say a fellow has been hijacking a lot of stuff, and he might confide in some fellow he thinks maybe is a friend. Say five of us pull a touch today, with a lot of stuff from a loft, such as clothing or silk or something. You put that into a warehouse. Naturally, by this one fellow telling this other fellow, this other fellow might get himself to go with his mob and say: "Listen, so and so left a lot of stuff in this place. It's going to lay in there until morning. How about if we beat it and get that stuff?" They get themselves together and get a truck, knowing it's a sure thing—although it leads to plenty of trouble, such as shooting. Naturally, they make an entrance into that place. What happens right here and then, they pull that stuff into another place, and they sell it. The warehouse people know that stuff is stolen. They don't do business with you. They do business with the fence.

Sometimes it comes out in the wash. They hold a conference and one guy accuses another, because I never yet seen a mob where they got beat for something, they would always see to blame what is known as the chump of the mob. They put the rap on him, probably take him out for a ride and torture him, to find out if he gave the tip on the stuff to some other friends of his.

If they can't get any information, they try to find out if he told anybody about it. The next move is to go and get this guy, watch him and try to con him. Probably he may tell somebody: "I just beat so and so for a lot of stuff." If you can, get around him and let him believe that you got confidence in him to be truthful with you. He can't even look you straight in the eye, knowing in his heart he's after beating you.

Maybe an argument may start some time or another, and he will come out with it. Or you probably take him out and try to get him drunk, or get a broad, until you get that information; and when you get the information, you take him and pick him up and put him in a car, and take him to a spot and torture him.

Maybe the rest of the mob will try to get the dough back—what they got for the stuff. You can forgive but never forget. It leads on to plenty of trouble.

Sometimes you can go in with fellows of your own mob and stick up a jewelry store, and everybody grabs stuff. You put it into your pockets and screw out. Maybe one fellow has a broad, and he wants to give her jewelry. When it comes to a split-up, he produces the stuff and shows it to a fence to be sold. Here a piece of jewelry is missing. You know that it's missing, but you can never find out. He may go to another fence and try to sell that jewelry, figuring, why should he get 400 when he can get 1500?

Right here he is beating you on your own end. That kind of a guy is better off dead than to be alive. He may probably get a good fellow to go to the chair for him, and who the hell is he to go to the chair for?

In this racket you can always find out, because it all comes out in the wash. You might find out maybe a week later: "So and so had a ring or brooch. He wanted to sell it to me, but he wanted too much money." Just for that minute they forget themselves, and how you find all your information is by people forgetting themselves. That kind of a guy is no good. They kill him.

You find cases like that in a lot of cases. Take a case where you are sticking up a crap game—probably the fellows that are doing the searching of the players. A good mob don't look to take anybody's watches or pins, because it's a bad move to take collat from crap games. You go looking to sell it, and right away you may get a pinch. Unless there's people there that's got a lot of jewelry—then take it too; but you don't find people there with thousands of dollars' worth of jewelry on them. When it comes for them to go to Police Headquarters, they are going to give a description of the watch and the ring, and a watch you got to throw overboard. That's the best move to make.

When you hold up a crap game, they go to the police about it. A thief don't like to be beat. He likes to beat everybody, but can't stand being beat himself. I myself never got beat by a mob, only by a broad. But nobody knows what's before them.

There are other ways that they get you and beat you. Take a case where you are very good friends with fellows that you know are racket guys. They know you are making money, and if they're not making it, they're jealous of you making money. What happens—they ain't got guts enough to go out and steal, they figure they will beat you and take you on a sure thing, knowing maybe they can square up with you by getting some of your good friends to square it up.

Here's a case I mean. Take a case where there's a lot of bonds involved. You may give them to a friend of yours to hold overnight, until morning, trying to get a connection to get rid of them. You don't know what's in his mind. You give him that stuff, having faith in him.

I did get beat once, myself, when I done a bit for a guy. He beat me for the money when I came out. I never seen him again to this day. I would kill him, because I actually done a bit for him. He didn't have nobody behind him, and I took the rap, figuring I would get a suspended sentence, but I got a rap. I had big people—H. B. Claflin—fighting against me.

By that time I was sixteen or seventeen years of age, I was a kid always had money, and making money every day by stealing trucks. I got called out in the hall by the District Attorney, who propositioned. If I stood trial, I would have been found guilty, and that way probably get a suspended sentence; but it's always business in them courts.

He propositioned—if I copped a plea, he would give me a lower plea and put a recommendation in for me. He was all right. It was a tough case. I was after getting pinched for six or seven times for the same kind of stuff. I had the Merchants' Protective Association fighting to send me away six or seven times. But this time they could have made a State and Federal case out of it.

Here's how they got me. I went and tried to beat the docks. I signed a fictitious name with my left hand to a bill of lading, to go down and pick up a load of stuff. I got the bill of lading. Then I looked for a job as driver or wagon boy with a silk house or dry-goods house.

I went to this here place. I was a skinny kid. The boss says to me: "You're too heavy for light work and you're too light for heavy work." But he gave me the job. I stole a couple of freight bills on him when he turned his head. I went to the dock, and the cashier of the Old Dominion Line—Pier 25, I think—on the North River. I went to them and they told me I needed a letterhead from the concern, and a written order to get the stuff. I went right back to the place, 229 Fourth Avenue, a silk house. The truckman I beat was a big corporation. They only ride silk and woolens. That time woolens was sky high.

I went right back to this here house that he did the trucking for. I said: "Hey, you didn't send down any letterhead or any order with this bill of lading." He said: "Yes, I sent one down, but go over to the girl and she'll give you another." I did, and she wrote out: "Please give to bearer . . ." and put the signature on it, and I got the stuff. I hired the truck from a friend of mine—a truckman.

I got pinched through a squeal, through jealousy, seeing that I wouldn't give up any dough to this guy or declare him in. One day I had stuff coming in. He was the only one that seen me and knew what I was doing. He telephoned the cops. They told me, the next morning, when business was being done, they told me that one of my own friends opened up on me. That's how I got pinched.

The guy I did the bit for—another fellow—got caught with me. I got the stuff from the Old Dominion Line myself, I didn't have him with me. I go and get this truckman to go with me, down to get this stuff. We have loaders down on the dock to throw the stuff on the truck. It was eleven cases. They threw the stuff on the truck. I paid them a better sum than what they asked for, and I signed the bill of lading with the Old Dominion Line checkers with my left hand, and I stole a Custom House License plate off another truck and put it on this automobile truck.

We got away with the stuff and drove to this place that was known as a drop-off, and put the stuff in there and went and got the truck away. In the meantime, I called up the fence and said: "I want to see you down in so and so's place," never mentioning what I got.

I went to this friend of mine and said: "Come on, kid, I got a good load." He said: "You're kidding." I said: "No, come on!" He was all dressed up, with a big diamond pin on. I got told by good friends that he was no good, to stay away from him; but I was going to split with him, because I liked him. I brought him down anyway. I says: "I want to open up them cases to see how much stuff is in there." In doing so, I looked to make as little noise as I could, because it draws attention.

Two guys came and knocked at the door, and they says: "Open up, John, I want to buy a horse and wagon," because there was a sign on the place that a horse and wagon was for sale. I went to the window to tell them the boss wasn't here and to come back tomorrow. I seen they were two bulls, and I jumped back to get away. I had all the doors locked and I couldn't get away. They got to the Polack in the next place, a big warehouse, and started firing shots. This fellow hiding near me says: "Come on, we better get out." Naturally, the bulls was looking all over the place—it was full of merchandise. I came out, and one of the bulls kicked me under the chin, and I fell. I was dressed like in working clothes, and the other fellow was all dressed up. They says to him: "You Jew bastard, what are you doing, sending this kid out to steal?" He was a few years older than me, and they felt he was using me for a tool, but I didn't give a God damn' for him. He listened to me. They pinched the both of us.

It shows it was a squeal, because why didn't they wait for the fence? This guy didn't squeal; he beat me on what I had. It's another fellow that squealed—jealousy. I guess he wanted to get rid of me, because he knew I wouldn't give up to him. I didn't have no use for him and he would come to me to take him out and try to get stuff, and I wouldn't play with him. He was the one that did it. I know it in my heart. The cops didn't tell me any names, but he was the only one that seen me that day.

When they asked: "Where did you get that stuff?" I told them I had a good alibi. I don't know where I got it. I told them: "I happened to be passing by this stable this morning and a man asked me if I wanted to go to work." I said: "Yes sir," and he told me I should take this truck and go over to the dock and pick up the stuff and bring it back, and if he wasn't here when I came back, wait until six o'clock and I will pay you. They said: "How did you get this fellow?" I said I told him to come on down and wait for me until I got paid, and we will go out and get something to eat.

They brought in the guy that owns the warehouse. They says: "Do you know this man?" I said: "No," and I knew him like a book. He said he didn't know me either. He said: "Listen, kid, stick right with me and I will get you out on bail." I said: "Don't worry about me, take care of yourself." I was certain to get convicted, so I copped a plea—pleading guilty to the charge.

They put this other kid on the stand first, and I seen the way the case was going that it looked real tough. Although I had two good lawyers. My lawyer called me out in the hall and says: "Kid, it will be a good idea to work on a plea and we can work for an s.s."—suspended sentence. At that time I had been out on three bails, and it looked real lousy. I said: "O.K.," and walked in and told the Court that this fellow was innocent, that I told him to come down and give me a hand. The jury went out, and came back in about five minutes and found him not guilty. The Judge refused to sentence me until I opened up. He took me into his chambers and I refused to listen to him. He held me for sentence.

In the meantime I had another case come up, that I got two and a half years in Sing Sing. It was account of a lot of sugar, that I didn't make a nickel on. My sentence was revoked.

Another way you can beat a dock is by going in and making a connection with a truck driver. You will give him so much for taking out this case, and he gets a pass from the checker O.K.ing him by the gateman.

As far as hijacking a truck, I wouldn't look to stop anybody from hijacking a truck, but what I would do is to take a good look at their faces, because right there it shows they are taking you on a sure thing. I would look to scheme them out, and sneak around after them to see where they come from, and after locating them I would know what to do with them. I would never look to make a holler to a cop, but would just look to get my own revenge for doing such a thing.

Or you can pull up with motorboats alongside of the dock and two fellows walk in on the dock, knowing that there's good stuff there, and throw the stuff right on to the motorboat, and screw away. You can pull right under the salutes—the piles—right under the dock.

You know how a ferry runway is hoisted up? Motorboats is pulled up there, and they drop that runway down in the night time. Underneath, there is a place like a warehouse, where they sell liquor. They do all their business at night when the ferry stops running at nine o'clock. I mean the ferries to Brooklyn. The boats aren't tied up on the New York side, they are on the Brooklyn side.

The cops know that. You can't conceal anything from them. If they see you coming with a case of booze, and they don't know you, they'll knock your brains out. They won't pinch you, because they know they will only hurt the people they are protecting. A strange guy, the cop tells him to go away from there. He knows what's going on. Either he is going to notify the people that is taking care of him and, naturally, they will send out one man to see who he is. If they know him it will be O.K., and if he's a fellow that's got any sense he stays away from that locality. Naturally, there are some people who are ignorant, and go down for a walk. If he looks suspicious, the cop will tell him: "What are you doing here?" and give him a frisk and chase him. Naturally, that party isn't coming back any more. But if he's looking for trouble, he can get all he wants.

Cops don't like them Federal Agents—they will give a tip that there's a Fed around. And Feds don't like cops. When they want to make an entrance, they got to go and get cops. The cop does the leading in and they do the arresting, but the cop ain't got no use for him.

The cop knows all this gang that's running it, he knows them all by sight. If he sees somebody that he knows doesn't belong there, he keeps an eye on them.

I was once shooting crap in a hotel where I was taking people, what is known as business people, in the said hotel. One time a couple of fellows happened to check in. They checked in single, they all checked in one at a time. Hearing a crap game is in session, they happened to come in, one by one.

I knew I was wanted for murder at that time. In fact, to be truthful, there was three of us wanted for murder of different people. We was always in the same hotel. I was pretty lucky in the mountains as to winning in crap games. Pretty near every night I always won $250 or $300, and I would walk away.

This here night I happened to be shooting crap. I was a youngster, but I had friends who were much older than me and knew dice better than I did, and 100 percent better than the gamblers of today, although they're dead. I happened to lose $450. Another friend of mine—he was also wanted for murder—happened to lose about $300. I figured: "Damn' it, I lost," and went away. Naturally, this friend of mine says: "Where do you come to shoot crap with these guys? Don't you see they're holding up the dice on you?" I didn't know, although I have been gambling since I was a kid. I like gambling better than a woman.

Nobody is smart, the best of them can be taken. I was always a hot-headed son of a bitch. "Are you sure I was taken?" He said: "Watch for yourself." I seen guys betting a hundred he's right—the guy with the dice. He would knock off two naturals, either a seven or an eleven. I observed it very carefully.

I said: "Son of a bitch, if I'm going to be taken by these bastards. I'm looking to chisel business guys up here, and these guys taking me for money. I'll stick them up and kill them for that $450." Because at that time one friend of mine was sending me money to pay my hotel bills and for my case. I said: "I'm going to stick them bastards up for my money." I went downstairs.

After they got through gambling, I found out their room, and walked up there and opened the door and held them up. They said: "What's the matter?" I said: "Walk out. I ought to take you out and blow your God damn' heads off." I said: "If you were regular guys, you wouldn't come in to take me." I said: "Why, you lousy punk." He said: "Please don't call me a punk." I banged him on the mouth and knocked all his teeth out, putting marks in my hand.

I walked them right down the stairs. Anyway, I took the money off them what I lost. I said to my friends: "What did you lose?" I didn't take a buck over what I lost. We was regular enough to give them back their money, and they said: "Thanks."

In the morning they came into the dining room. The fellow I busted the night before, I talked to him, and I says: "How are you feeling, fellow?" I didn't think enough to ask to pay his bill. I know better now. I said: "How are you feeling, anyway?" He said: "O.K." I said: "If you guys stay here, we'll make plenty of money." They skipped out and never came back.

A couple of fellows came to me one night and says: "Listen, do you want to go and drive a car in this here game? It's a sure thing." I said: "No." I never look to step in and clip a crap game, because maybe them guys might come to my crap game and recognize me.

They proceeded and made the game and they shot a guy in the arm, and a guy got shot on their side. They took him and had him fixed up. That's how they got pinched later.

I says: "No, I don't like to go out to stick up any crap games." Anyway, they proceeded and they did it.

About two hours after they stuck up the game, there was a fellow that was in our mob that was known as a steerer, and a no-good son of a bitch. Nobody trusted him. People say till today that he was afraid of me. He would say: "That Irishman is crazy, he'll step up and kill you for nothing, that guy." I gave the impression that I didn't give a damn' for nobody, as far as fighting is concerned. My friends always told me: "Don't go out with him, or don't take any walk with him." I always turned him down, figuring he might give me a steer.

One night he says: "Where you walking?" I says: "Towards so and so." He says: "I'm going that way." I can't say: "I don't want to go with you." To my opinion, he would kill a man without a murmur, either. To tell you the truth, I liked him to a certain degree, but I never figured he was looking to steer me.

On that night I won't say he was looking to steer me. I was going for coffee myself, and he suggested: "You want to have some coffee?" I said: "O.K." We went into a restaurant and in walks these guys. I says: "Listen, so and so, I know I'm going to be taken, but do me a favor and kill this so and so, because he steered me."

I seen everybody step in with their hands in their pockets and figured I was going to be taken.

My face was white, because I figured: "They are a mob from some city or another that's stepped in, and if they see so and so they're going to kill them."

I said: "If you can sneak out of here, sneak out and come back with two guns." He did happen to sneak out. It made me more suspicious. I knew I couldn't run out, because I would be stopped with about thirty bullets. So I sat there.

A guy happened to be looking at me. He says: "Don't you remember me from the mountains?" I seen a whole mouth of gold teeth. I said: "What part of the mountains?" I said: "Oh, yeah." He says: "Don't you remember what happened there?" I said: "Why talk about it, it's so long ago? Why don't you forget it?" He happened to say: "Don't you remember, we happened to be shooting crap and you busted me?" That made me more suspicious. I said to myself: "That bastard, he's got me set up nice." I said to myself: "If he ever gets back with them guns, I'll kill him first and then these fellows."

Anyway, me and this feller had a conversation. I said: "Aw, forget about it." He says: "Sure." He says: "Maybe you can get back that money? You know so and so. They took the game and maybe you could get the money." I said: "Yeah, I'll see if I can get the money." I wanted to sneak out and try to meet this friend who went after the guns.

I told them I would go. Outside I met my friend, with the guns. He says: "O.K." I said: "Give me the two guns." He said: "No, I'm going in with you." I stepped into the restaurant and I knew they acted different. I said to myself: "Use your head, these guys happened to be stuck up in a game and they want their money back." There was one fellow, I didn't like his face. He said: "Go ahead." I said: "No, go ahead you, go out."

They never got their money back but anyway three of the guys that stuck up the game are dead today. They got theirs in other stickups.

Chapter 12
PULLING A PHONY PINCH

A rapper's a man that's been robbed, or something stolen from him. They gain his confidence and look to push the rap over on you, and if it's a man with a record, that man has got to do plenty of explaining to get himself out.

I was once picked up where a man identified my picture in Police Headquarters for a jewelry robbery, where the jeweler got shot and he picked out my picture. I happened to be in a bondsman's office that day and the following day. The following day two detectives came up and says: "Hey, you, we want you for a rap." I said: "What the hell are you talking about—what kind of a rap?" He says: "A stickup." He says: "Do you want to come over and give yourself up, or do you want us to take you?"

I knew one of them was looking to give me a break, but I knew I didn't do it, and the bondsman knew it too, and a couple of other people that happened to be real estate people at the time of the robbery. Here they were, looking for an Irishman, a Jew and a Wop, and the combination happened to be there. They took us into the station house.

I got brought into the station house, to the detectives' room, and they brought in a witness—one of the people that had been stuck up—and they made us change clothes. What I mean is, taking off your soft hat and putting on a peaked cap, which might have been like the guy in the robbery, but I didn't know nothing about it. They brought in the man and tried to tell him: "That's him, the guy that's coughing." I was real sick with a bad cold and I wouldn't go to bed, because I was a fellow that would never give in to sickness. My motto is, if you are going to die, you will die.

The guy says: "No, I could recognize the fellow that stuck me up ten years from now." They proceeded to take us to the hospital to see the other man, that was shot at the robbery. They failed to identify me, although they identified my picture at headquarters. I says to myself: "These bums are looking for money."

I happened to have on a big diamond pin and a diamond ring, and they says: "Gee, kid, you look like you're in the dough!" They said: "I hear you won seven thousand in a crap game." I said:

"Maybe I did, but you don't hear what I lost." They said: "Loan us your pin." I said: "What the hell do you want that pin for?" I wouldn't give it to him. He says to me: "That's nice collat you got on there." I had a receipt to show I bought it—I never wear stolen jewelry. I turned around and says to myself: "I'm going to hock this pin and ring because it might get me in trouble." Anyway, with a little argument we got out of the station house. They were looking to hold us for forty-eight hours, but seen they were getting into a lot of trouble. One cop got suspended account of the whole thing, and got put into a uniform, and got put out in a section where it took him plenty of time to get home.

I once got a pickup while waiting for a truckload of beer in a part of Brooklyn, where a cop jumped on the running board and stuck my friends and I up, and got inside the car and says: "Drive to the station house." I never like the idea in going to a station house. I would always look to do business with the cop while on the way. I says: "What are you picking me up for?" He says: "Because you look suspicious to me." I says: "I'm waiting here for somebody." He says: "Tell me who." I says: "Well, go on ahead, I ain't going to name no names. That's how much you're going to know at the end, anyway."

He held the three of us up with his gun. He took us in to the station house and called down the inspector of detectives and a captain of detectives also. They got us inside, asked who owned the car. I told them: "I don't know who owns it." He says: "Well, who are these here guys?" I says: "I happened to meet them in a theatre and got introduced to them. Only thing I know about them is that they are bootleggers." He says: "And what are you, the protection guy?" Knowing that I got a record, that is what they figured me for. I didn't see any sense giving them an alias, because I knew I would be recognized by doing so. Figured I would save that smack on the chin and give them my right name.

I was waiting for a truck. If I thought they had something on me, I would shoot it out with him right there. Either he'd take me or I'd take him. There happened to be a lot of shooting going on in Brooklyn, guys getting killed; and, naturally, they had suspicions of us, because when they asked how many times was you ever arrested, I admitted and told them: "Yes, about eighteen or nineteen times"—at that time. I guess that made them more suspicious that we were desperate characters, and maybe out for something else.

Right here the captain of detectives came in, and they had rubber pipes out, and he says: "Well, you bums, you better talk." I had done nothing and I didn't talk, and my friends didn't either, because they didn't have nothing on us.

Then the captain of detectives came down and questions us one by one. First he called in the other two friends of mine, knowing that they had no record, and on calling them in separately, he says: "What are you doing here?" They said: "We're bootleggers." They won't lock you up for that. He asked them also where they happened to meet me. They told him that they happened to get introduced to me in a theatre one night, and whenever they got stuff in they would call on me, to throw a buck my way. Between you and I, I was never no protection guy for nobody and never carried a gun for nobody, as I hate a dictator. Just because you think you were somebody, why the hell should I carry a gun for you?

Anyway, the captain called me in and says to me: "Listen, what are you doing here in Brooklyn?" I told him: "Waiting for a truckload of beer." He says: "What kind of truck is it?" I says: "A green truck with a certain name on it"—which was a lie. He told the cops to go out and wait for such a truck. I could have laughed my head off when he did so. If they thought I would tell them the truth, they were out of their heads. He said: "Where did you meet these fellows?" I told the same story as they had told him. He says to the detectives: "These guys are O.K. They are only bootlegging." That's no crime, as long as the cops don't bother you.

We got put in cells at another station house and held overnight to appear in court. Then a guy comes in and says to me: "I'm a bondsman and I got sent down to help you." I said: "I don't know you—don't name no names—I don't know you." Right after that a couple of coppers brought in what is known as phony rappers—somebody that's been stuck up and probably been robbed—and they'll look sometimes and make a mistake, and identify you instead of the real ones that did it. They'll say: "Yes," and you will say: "No," and they will have more faith in them than in you because they know you have a record. They ain't got any belief in you whatsoever.

Here's what happens. It's either a case of dough, if they know you are making money, and they want it. Knowing you went through the racket so much, they will look to pin such a thing on you. We got brought before the lineup in the morning. Naturally, these two friends of mine, the cops happened to find out that they had records. They told the cops the night before they were never pinched. The captain says: "Here's three men that has been picked up at such a street and I myself questioned them." He says: "I will tell you right here and now, these fellows are big operators in the booze"—meaning the other two—and he pronounced me a protection guy for them. I just didn't say anything, and they kept quiet. They held us to last and looked us over real good. Got brought before a Judge in a Magistrate's Court.

In the meantime we had obtained a counselor, but our case got postponed for 48 hours. One copper says: "Listen, where do you come from?" I told him where I come from. He says: "Do you know so and so?" I said: "What's the use of mentioning names, I won't tell you if I knew them or didn't." He says: "No, kid, you look like a regular guy, and I will help you out." I guess he figured I'm a money guy, and he'd get money. We didn't do any business with him, but my lawyer came in and says: "Listen, I got to have so and so much money." I says: "For what?" He says: "For the cops." Which was always my motto, "live and let live," but not as far as a copper; but you got to give up. Naturally, we produced that much money—all except, I believe, one hundred and fifty dollars. We were arraigned in Court 48 hours later, and they had a phony rapper there, and he told us: "I'm going to give you a break, but if youse ain't got the rest of that money by six o'clock," he says, "I got another rap for you guys." Knowing that we didn't do such a thing, or do anything in fact, but it was a case of giving up dough—that was all to do.

We didn't get discharged. The Judge was still sore on account of my having a record. He wanted to hold us another 48 hours. Our counselor put up a fight to have us discharged. The Judge proceeded in holding us for another 48 hours. In the meantime we obtained a writ. Inside of two hours we were brought down to the Supreme Court and arraigned before a Supreme Court Judge. In Brooklyn you got to go higher than the police—which is another case of more dough because, boy, between you and I, they don't step for nothing. What I mean is, to come to Court as quick as they should do. Everything is, you got to put up on the line. It was a case of putting bail on us.

The Supreme Court Judge, he was asked by the District Attorney to put a low bail on us. He put a God damn' low bail on the three of us, and we happened to get out an hour later, but to appear again in the Magistrate's Court within 48 hours, which we did, and the sitting Magistrate all through the case praised the lawyer in our case for doing the work that he did, by getting us a writ and having us out, and now to be discharged. But, boy, it takes dough to do that kind of thing. As I will say and always will say, that it is always the unfortunate who suffers. My friends raised the dough for me; the other two fellows, they had dough. These other two fellows would have put it up, which they did.

In my opinion, the best Police Commissioner there has been in New York was Police Commissioner Enright. Because he was noted, as far as the underworld was concerned, as a good man. He was not too strict with the cops that were under him, and a cop was not so afraid as he is today. Today, with Whalen, when a cop shoots a man, he gets a medal the next day, and is made a detective.

A Chief of Police in a certain city was once held in the Federal Court, as his friend got knocked off. I happened to know him. He liked me a lot. We had a little conversation. There was a kid on trial that got caught with a lot of booze. He was found guilty. The Chief of Police said to him: "You son of a bitch, you should learn to tell more lies, not the truth." He said to me one day: "We are going to hold automobile races. If you want a concession to sell frankfurters, etc., I will see that you get the concession." I said: "Have you got any jewelry stores that I can stick up?" It was only a town with 5,000 population. He said: "If there was a jewelry store, I would stick it up myself."

Plenty times cops set out to get habitual criminals, to frame them. Take the case of Gerald Chapman and leading criminals. A kid like Chapman, I know, never did what he got killed for. I know he was too smart to do such a thing. They were just looking to get him out of the way. If something gets pulled, they say so and so pulled that trick—like one that escapes from prison. If he ever does get caught, they will convict him on that thing. The jury is prejudiced against him, too, because of his reputation. In Chapman's case, he was convicted on account of his reputation and his character, that was all. I am sure he never did that. He would steal and steal without a gun.

Supposing somebody got shot here. They would probably pick me up and have somebody identify me. They look to pick me up, and they will. There is no question about it. And they will charge me with the murder, and I will have to prove myself innocent. You must have plenty of money to beat it.

A guy steps out on the corner, another guy steps up to him, shoots him, jumps into a cab, goes up Third Avenue. You step out of here on to the street. The cop would go after the guy that did it. He might figure that I was implicated, and pick me up too. I might not know anything about it. But I would have to do some good explaining to get myself out of it. I would have to get you to prove that I just left your house. They would come right down to your house and question you. They would pick you up and hold you as a witness. They take you bodily if you object, and put you through a third degree.

Chapter 13
BEATING A FRAMEUP

That time, out in the Middle West—the cops knew I got shot through a political fight, so they questioned me, and I refused to answer their questions. They called me a liar, and I told them I thought they were damn' fools for questioning me. They said to me: "How do you know so and so?" I said: "Well, I was introduced to him." They said: "What was you doing in the hotel with him?" I said: "What is that your business? That is my business." I know that man is the leading politician there and he is a good man, and why should I turn on that man? I said: "The only thing I know is that he is a respectable man and a lawyer." They said: "What kind of business have you with him?" I said: "I have no business with him. I know he is a respectable business man." They know he is one of the biggest bootleggers in that city. I didn't tell it to any court to be recorded in any minutes.

They brought this man for me to try to identify him. They were looking to frame him. That fellow was too good of a fellow to put me on the spot. I happened to be with other fellows, and they gave out information as to my whereabouts. They told the cops. They happened to bring this fellow in. I had a date with this fellow to go to a cabaret. He went to his home for supper and I met him later in the evening.

After my being shot I was brought to a hospital. Ten minutes later they brought in this fellow, and they thought I was going to die. I said: "You dirty bunch of bums, do you want to frame that man?" It's a good thing I held my head. I always remember what I am doing. "That is not the man that shot me. You dirty bums, don't hurt him in any way." He said: "They are not knocking me around." He had an argument with one of the detectives. They held him under a bond of $10,000.

They didn't believe me. They locked all my friends up, and a friend that was after giving me a quart of blood, and it was a shame. They charged them as suspicious persons. They tried to accuse them that they shot me. If it was not for them, I would probably be dead. They brought me to the hospital.

They all got sentenced to time in prison, with the exception of one. They got 30 days and costs, and a fine besides. They got charged with suspicious persons. One fellow happened to get discharged. They were looking to question them as to who shot me. I asked them not to say anything. They did so, all right. They could not get away any more. All the cops happened to come in. They questioned those fellows. I know one thing in my heart, even if they would have squealed, I would say: "That is not the man." I would help him, and not see him go to jail, even if I was to die. He would probably get the chair, and I would never do it.

Well, there were six cops placed on detail to watch me in the hospital. They would always question me. I asked them not to ask me any of those questions about politicians, because I am not in condition to talk to them. I knew I would be well taken care of.

Out there in that city a big political fight was going on, and a big investigation. They said: "This guy is here from New York to kill some councilman." A councilman through the West is like a state senator in this city. They accused me of all those things. I didn't care what they said. It didn't worry me.

The District Attorney's Office is the only office that the opposite side held. All account of him I got held in jail, and to tell you the truth, I got kidnapped out of the hospital. I was not discharged. The cops took me out. The cops were regular with me, but it was orders with them. They knew that I could do something, probably, for them, and which they asked me. They said: "Maybe you can speak to so and so for me." This man had been accused of getting cops on the force, and he was a man known as to get cops broke. He was one of the leading politicians, and they knew I was on the good side with him, and they figured that they would get me to talk to him to help them. I took it all in, and if I could help them I would.

Anyway, I was brought to Court. I was treated 100 percent. They first put me in a cell and took good care of me. They said: "You are not a rat, anyway. When you get out there will be plenty of bloodshed. I guess you will clean up this city." I was too smart. I said: "I don't know who shot me. Probably I got shot by mistake." Anyway, they held me on a charge of defraud. I laid in the can for fourteen days. I was treated 100 percent there. I got anything I wanted. I got brought before the Homicide Bureau and questioned as to what I was doing in this city. I said I was visiting friends. They started pumping questions at me as to the politicians, but I was too smart. I would not answer.

They charged me with defrauding an innkeeper. If I didn't have people behind me, I probably would get one to three years. The hotel got paid afterwards. I had a leading district attorney of Cleveland as one of my lawyers.

I got put on a tier that was known as Murderers' Row. I was not the chap that would make a holler. If I had the worst pain in the world I would not let anyone know. Why do they want to know my pain? They can't help me. Well, I'll tell you the truth. I was placed in a cell in the Police Headquarters, and it was a cold, cold place, and I knew that if I would stay there I would kick in. I figured: "What is the good of hollering? I guess I am getting the works." I kept my mouth shut, but the detective that was interested in my case came up and took me out, and I slept in a private room. That room was better furnished than the room in my own home. I had my meals shipped in, and that you can't get in that city. I got anything I wanted. The cops even wanted to pay for my meals. They say that I had leading people coming up, and that I knew leading people. I said: "O.K., Chief, you need not pay for that." They got papers for me to read, and books.

Then I was brought to the Police Headquarters for questioning after I got out of the hospital, and was brought before the Judge. The cops went to the front for me. They said everything was paid in the hotel, that I was not wanted in any other city for a crime. The Judge said to me: "What are you doing here?" I was bent over. I said: "Your Honor, I just came out to visit some friends." He said: "It was a bum visit." I said: "Yes." He said: "Who shot you?" I said: "I don't know." The District Attorney said: "Your Honor, this man was arrested about 20 times and he is nothing but an Eastern gangster, and I want him to be held on a high bond for a charge of defraud." That Judge would have discharged me if it had not been for that District Attorney, but I guess he was instructed to dig in to me and get revenge on me for the politicians that he was in trouble with.

I got brought to the County Jail and placed in a cell with two fellows. I could not sleep that night, and when the doctor came around I said: "My stomach hurts me like anything." My testicles hurt me on account of being shot in the stomach, so much that I couldn't hardly walk, and it gave me a lot of pain. He said: "Lay down in bed and put an ice bag on you." The doctor came around in the morning and said: "How are you feeling?" I always said: "O.K., Doc." The next thing you know, he said: "Take your clothes and go downstairs." He said: "You'll have to go down. I don't know how to cure you."

I was told at Police Headquarters by the cops and by the leading members of the Police Department they liked me very much. They said: "I never trusted a crook or a gangster in my life, but, kid, you are one nice kid, and I'll go to hell for you. You got pretty good people calling me up and going to the front for you. Don't worry, you will be treated better in the County Jail."

On my arrival there I got the works, because the sheriff of the City of Cleveland happened to be against the side that I was with. So I got the works, all right. They treated me lousy. They would feel happy if I died. But when I felt sick I would fight it off. One thing is, I was tickled to death that no politicians came in to see me, because it would be a bad move for them. Then they began to treat me better. My cell was never closed, only after 9 o'clock at night, but I got anything I wanted. The sheriff would call me up and say: "The Boxing Commissioner was asking for you and sends his regards." They read so much about me. Probably they had been introduced to me, but I forgot their names. I would say that I don't think that I knew of them.

Anyway, they have what is called a true bill or a no bill. That is as far as indictments go. I was told not to worry, that everything would be taken care of. They generally indict you within a week, out there, but I knew everything would be taken care of.

When I was left go out of the County Jail it was a snowy day. It was snowing and sleet. I went for my clothes at Police Headquarters. I tell you the truth, there were ties, shirts and suits missing. I did not make a holler, but I said to myself: "Them cheap bastards! But, what the hell, they are only cops. Maybe they need it. Let them keep it." I did not trust myself any more with them. Maybe I would get picked up again.

I was going out of town and found out that there were no trains going straight to New York City, but they told me there was a train leaving for Buffalo and that I could make connections from Buffalo to go on to the city. I was getting trailed all the time, and I happened to recognize them in the station. I took the train, and when I arrived in Buffalo two bulls patted me on the back. I guess they were notified from Cleveland. I was not hard to pick up. I was badly bent over. I did not have the bullets removed. I just had one extracted and am going back again to get out the others that are in my body.

When I stepped off the train in Buffalo they patted me on the back. I did not believe they were cops until a uniformed cop came over to me. To tell you the truth, there are guys that pull copper rackets. They can always get those kinds of uniforms, and I didn't trust them. Then I first believed that they were real cops, and they said to me: "You will have to make this train." I was figuring on staying in Buffalo that night. But they told me that I had a half hour to catch the next train. They would not let me get out of the station. I had to eat in the station. They kept a close watch on me, and when I came out of the restaurant, they saw to it that I took the train, and they did not leave me until the train pulled out of the station.

When I arrived in New York, I was met by more cops. I told them: "Do you think I would be a fool to carry a gun?" They said: "If you want to do shooting, don't do any in this city, go out of the city." I said: "What do you think I am, a Jesse James?" Then I came home around my section, and all the cops would say: "Jesus Christ, you better stay away from that city, you got it bad." Everybody thought I was dead. There were rumors around that my body had been brought home dead. But I fooled them. I am still here. I got shot for mixing in the political racket. I would do it again.

Out in Cleveland I was in a pay hospital, a very good hospital, and was treated very good. I got anything I wanted. The doctors were O.K., and the cops were looking to get me out. Then they cut the six detectives down to three. That is a big bunch to watch a man when they can send me to a city hospital. Then they removed me to a city hospital, with the bullets in my body yet. I couldn't move. I was just bent over. But I had a smile on my face. The Captain of Police was very nice to me. He said: "Hello, kid," and I said: "Hello, Cap." I told him I did not feel so good. He says: "Don't think that I am a bad fellow, I am a good fellow." I said: "I know, Cap. I ain't saying nobody is a bad fellow." He treated me very nice and offered me cigarettes. He instructed his men this way. They were going to move me in a police patrol.

I knew that I was getting the works by being sent to the city hospital. That was the politician's racket on the other side, as to my removal. There was another fellow in the same private room with me, and why didn't they ship him to a city hospital? He was feeling better than I was. They were only interested in shipping me to that hospital. I said: "I guess I got to take it." I took it. The Captain was very nice towards me, and he said to his men: "Listen, I like this kid and, another thing, I want you to take it very easy going over them roads with this kid, because this kid is in no condition to be jarred in that patrol wagon. Another thing, take it very easy, and cover him up good with plenty of blankets." I said: "Gee, Cap, I don't think I can lay down straight." I was in a position of a 45-degree angle.

A couple of friends of mine came in to visit me, and an official from a big cab company out there, and he liked me a whole lot. He said: "How are you feeling?" I said: "O.K." He said: "We tried to hold you in this hospital, but I will see that you are taken care of and that you are shipped back here." The Captain said: "Are you a good friend of his?" He said: "Yes." The Captain said: "Do you want to go and hire a private ambulance?" This friend of mine said: "Yes, I will." To tell you the truth, it nearly made me cry when I saw the way the Captain treated me. I said: "Thank you very much, Captain." He said: "That's O.K., kid, I don't care what you are. You look to me like a nice kid." I said: "Don't think because I have a record I am a bad fellow myself." He said: "That's O.K., kid."

My friends called a private ambulance, which they paid for. There was a cop placed with me to take me to the City Hospital out there. I was brought into that hospital, and a lousy orderly that made himself more important than the doctor—I guess he didn't like my face, or maybe I won some of his money—he goes and puts me in a prison ward. All the cops were interested in me there. They knew what I was shot for.

It was a living graveyard. I didn't care if I died or if I didn't die. I was placed in a cold, cold room all by myself, and I couldn't hardly breathe. When the nurse would come, she would give me an argument. One thing, in my heart, I know if I was on my feet I wouldn't care how they treat me. If a man is laying in bed, a person should look to help a person, especially when he is sick. Anyway, I used to get visits there, and to get my visits my friends had to go to a station house, because the cops would not let them in unless they had a pass from the station house. I laid in bed, and the only time I got any attention was on that night. A doctor came around and took a pedigree of me, as to my name, etc. Well, that night he dressed me. The next day I found out that he is a leader in an orchestra in Cleveland and that he was going through to be a doctor.

To tell you the truth, his mind was not on being a doctor, because even the nurses told me later that he don't care for that profession. He came around one day and I was real sick, after complaining to the cops and nurses. He came around and I said: "Do something for me." He said: "Give him a pill." I said: "Doc, will you please put a dressing on my stomach?" He said: "That will be all right. I will dress you tomorrow morning." I said: "Doc, I am in your care. Do whatever you want."

I laid in bed there for about a week and a half. All my meals were ice cold. The only thing I was living on was milk and crackers. Well, it was a living graveyard, and that's the truth. There was one nice nurse. Two of the three orderlies happened to be good fellows. I never liked the third orderly. The other two orderlies said to me: "You look like a damn' nice fellow."

One day the doctors came around and I said: "Gee, Doc, you're treating me like a dog." I said: "I can't breathe." They told me I was going to lose one of my legs. They told me they would work on me the next day and operate on me. I said: "O.K., Doc." I was willing to sign any papers as far as the operation goes. The nurse came around that day and said: "Listen, here is a bath robe.

Get up and get on a wheel chair." I was surprised to hear that. I got on the wheel chair. I tried to walk and I walked pretty good. The next day they took the wheel chair away from me, and I was told to walk, which I did. I walked, and there was a little colored girl there and she was also being held as a prisoner, and I used to talk to her. The cops were O.K. with me there in the hospital. They would mail letters for me. They did everything they could for me.

The next thing, the day I was to be operated on, two cops came to me and said: "Dress up, you have to go to the can today." So I went. Anyway, going out in the patrol wagon, I said: "Take it easy, my stomach is wide open." They moved me without underwear or anything—just a suit of clothes. As to my underwear, I didn't want to wear it. It was full of blood. It was cut off of me. I threw it away.

I got to the can. It was a living graveyard. I would not want to see a dog lay there. I stayed in the can fourteen days until I came up for a hearing, and I was discharged.

They always told me that I got shot with steel bullets. I believed it too, because I know that lead will only set into poison.

I went to a cabaret and I felt pretty good, until about two weeks. One Sunday morning my stomach started to swell up, and I went to a hospital. The doctors would not let me out. They said: "What is the matter?" I said: "I had been shot." I said I still had three bullets in me. I was admitted to the hospital, and my stomach burst open. The doctors and nurses worked on me and I had good attention. I had a bullet removed without ether or anything. I don't like drugs. It might lead to a habit.

I knew I was in good hands. I knew I was being treated by good doctors. They got one bullet out. I saw they made a good cut of it. It hurt a lot, but better out than in. They x-rayed my stomach. They x-rayed today and tomorrow. The bullet would move. I have to go to the hospital again and get the rest of the bullets taken out of my body.

The next day after my operation, I was just coming out of ether, a fellow was coming up to see me. He said: "If you need any money, I got plenty of money." He pulled out a big bankroll, which can be proven. He laid the money on my bed in Mount Sinai Hospital in Cleveland. He said: "I will stand the expense." He asked me who shot me, and told me: "I'll get even for you. I know you don't even remember meeting me. You must be in a coma now." I said: "I don't want your money. Just bring me up a bottle of soda," which he did. I drank it quickly.

That day they gave me up and told me I was going to die. They would not let any people in to see me. That is how I got pneumonia. I started to vomit, and I vomited blood and had the room flooded. They started rushing pans to me. I didn't bleed much externally from being shot in my stomach. They gave me up that day. They said: "You drank a soda." I said: "No, Doc, I didn't drink anything." "Don't tell me," he said, "it looks like a dark soda." Afterwards I admitted it. Then he grabbed ahold of the fellow who was visiting me and this fellow hit him. The cops asked me who that fellow was, but, to tell the truth, to this day I don't know who he is. The only thing I can say, he is a damn' good regular fellow. They said: "Maybe he is up here to kill you." But I knew he was not.

Later on I found out that he was looking to connect me with his mob. I could tell by his ways. He never came to see me any more, but always used to call the hospital and tell the nurses to give his best regards, and if I needed anything that they should let him know over the phone. I got treated 100 percent pretty good. As far as the gambling and vice people are concerned, there were people coming up to see me that I never met in my life. They used to come up with flowers around my bed. But I ain't dead yet, and I didn't need any flowers—why go to that expense? All the girls used to come up. They would say to me: "Gee, kid, I like you." I would say: "Why go to the expense of bringing me stuff?" But they said: "I know so much about you, that you are a regular fellow." I never took anything from a woman in my life, and here they used to bring up cigarettes and so on. I am a fellow that never even took a handkerchief from a girl, and everyone that knows me can verify that statement. It was too bad that I could not see those people on the day that I got out of the can. If I ever meet them, I will treat them better than they had ever treated me.

About forgeries—they have already charged and told me that I was a forger. The Burns guys were looking high and low for me for a couple of months. They were figuring they would get me. Although on my arrest they told me they knew where I was, but they didn't want to go to the bother of coming out there. I know I would make a holler and fight extradition. I knew in my heart that I never did cash a check or ever make out a check. Unless I knew that it was a good check, I would never look to cash it. But they didn't want to know that. They wanted to get the low-down. They happened to pinch me on my being discharged for a charge of highway robbery. I got re-arrested in the same court room, and brought before the Inspector.

The cop that pinched me was told not to hit me. He said: "O.K., I'll see that he don't get touched." I was brought to the Inspector's office and questioned as to the checks. I said: "I'll admit cashing those checks, that is my signature, but I didn't know they were phony checks. If I did, I would not have cashed them." They were for about $15,000, about 35 checks. I got them in a crap game. He didn't want to know that. So he says to me: "Who is this guy so and so?" mentioning the name. I said: "He used to shoot crap with me." Anyhow, I would not identify anybody that he brought in front of me. Why should I get him in trouble? I never like company in any of my arrests, and I didn't want to see anybody else get arrested. The Burns people used to take me for breakfast down in the corridor of the Criminal Courts Building.

I engaged one of the leading counsel, and he said to me: "O.K., I'll see you at the court in the morning." He did come down, and I explained to him the whole case, and he said: "O.K." I got a bad record, and through my record they were working on that theory. They were trying to hang something on me. Anyway, my case was postponed and postponed and postponed between several Magistrates at different hearings, until one day there was a tough Magistrate sitting on the bench, and my lawyer made them open up law books, and I got discharged. My lawyer brought out that I would not cash a phony check. I was never held on such a charge before. Why should I do it to a friend of mine? The bank got stuck. The bank people could not identify me that I ever cashed a check, but they compared writings, and they tried to hold me as an accessory to the crime of forgery.

After a long while before the Magistrate, I admitted cashing a check, all right, and he asked me if I cashed checks for any amounts of money, and I said: "Yes, because I am a gambler and I am looking to win the money." He said: "Do they pay you any sum of money for cashing the check?" I said: "I don't charge them any money for cashing the check, but they sometimes stake me to five dollars for cashing a check, or probably a couple of cigars." They say: "Here is five dollars—get a cigar."

Chapter 14
HOW TO COMMIT A MURDER—

Supposing I got trouble with you and want to get you. I would treat you nice, would "hello" you, and look to keep right in your path and watch every move you make. See where you go, see who your friends are, and see what streets you walk through, and this or that, and then I would plan to meet you the best way to clip you without getting pinched. I might try to scheme you out with a girl.

I got a fight with you. You're one gang, I'm another gang. The best move to make is if I would see you outside I would kill you.

The best way to kill a man is not to confide in anybody. Keep it just between yourself—you can't trust everybody. He might have somebody in my own gang giving him information that I'm looking to clip him. I would look to see where he lives, or if he had an automobile I would put a piece of dynamite in his starter and blow him up in his car; or try to blow up his house. I would scheme another way, how to get a girl. I would get a broad to make him and give him a steer for me. I would take him that way, or else scheme him through her to give him a walk, and when he walks with her pick him up and throw him into a car. Take him and torture him. Find out who is steaming him up on me. When he gives that information, kill him.

If I had trouble with a man, wherever I would see him I would kill him. I'd take a chance. Don't care if I burn in the chair or not. Wouldn't care if it was in the Palace Theatre or anywhere else.

The real point how to commit a murder is always use your head and scheme a man out. Have a little patience, and you can get him in a right spot. Sometimes, if you got plenty of money, you can set him up in a cabaret. You can plan a space, and have one wall with a curtain the dead image of the two opposite walls. When he enters the place, have him set up to sit so and so, and while he is sitting there you can blow his brains out. If others are with him, kill them that are with him, too, and make sure they are all out of the way.

It's always best to use your head and work with the cops, make connections for yourself and move around and meet people and do favors for them same people, without any money, because

137

some time you are going to go to them for a favor, and they got to do that favor for you—which I can assure is being done right now in the Police Department.

In some cases there is real tough nuts where the guy you want to get, if he has a gun, is going to shoot it out with you. So the only way to handle him is to let him linger and you stay low. Don't leave yourself in any position where he can go and clip you, and always have somebody to try to keep in contact with him as to his whereabouts, where he lives, and if he gambles, where he gambles. Naturally, he is sure to gamble. Ninety-nine percent of them gamble.

Your next move is to pull a connection with that crap game, and to get a friend of yours to get a job in that crap game as doorman or diceman or something, and he knows what he is instructed to do. He is a friend with everybody in the game, although everybody has a little suspicion of him; but he uses his head and tries to convince them same people that he is not against them.

He holds such position, until one night he is instructed: "When so and so come to the door, let them in." They will take off as cops. He has a good description of them, he is told to let them in, because he knows his life is at stake if they don't get in—unless it is a fatal error of the cops or somebody else. Because sometimes cops come into the game for money.

He is instructed to holler: "Cops!" The fellow that is running the game figures the cops busted in on him while he is letting in a player. Naturally, the people who have guns on them ditch them, so the cops don't catch the said guns on their persons. Naturally, you have a fellow who is walking with you and is standing right next to him. The fellow that they want is marked for death and he points a finger. That finger meaning so and so. Naturally, they take off as cops, they say: "We don't want to pinch the bunch—who's running the game?" The fellow who is running steps up and says: "I am." They take him out bodily and talk to him in the street, and then say: "Why talk in the street, let's go in here," and take him to some restaurant. Then they stick handcuffs on him and put him in a car and take him some place and torture him to death, after they get what they want out of him.

In this here racket nobody is too careful. Them bullets don't care who you are. The man who kills him would have plenty of money behind him in order to get out. While he is in prison nobody can kill him, as he is too careful with his meals. I guess he has all his meals shipped in to him, or probably has his own cook, as he can well afford it. Poison, that's a good way of killing a man while he is in prison—which I have seen. Suppose an enemy of yours is in the can—in the Tombs Prison awaiting trial. It would be a very clever idea, when somebody should get pinched, to pull a connection with him and have a dinner sent in consisting of chicken, apples, and so forth, and don't eat them, but distribute them to him—just being his friend in prison, which everybody likes to be a friend. When you give it to him, it is known as slow poison—you don't feel the effects until it reaches your heart, and then you can't go any more.

I was at one time doubled up in the same cell with a rat, a fellow that I knew was a rat, who sent somebody to Sing Sing for twenty years. I tried to pull a connection with my friends, saying I would kill him if they would put up so much money. I was foolish at that time and would have done it if the money was produced, knowing that I needed money for my own case.

I was in my cell for murder at that time, and he was held for murder also, for shooting some fellow in the mouth and killing him—a union leader. Every day my friends came down, I would talk to them to get connections with a certain party which I knew very well, and I know I would have killed him by having a bottle of booze shipped in and letting him drink it, and kill him that way. If not, I would have got up ahead of him in the morning and cut his throat and walk out; naturally, knowing I would have been held for the same charge, but which I would have denied; and I know I would get away with it.

I would have a knife shipped in, which I know can be done for two dollars or less. Pull a connection with a fellow doing time for sixty or ninety days, and they would get me the knife for the sum of two dollars, through a package of clothes or something. You can always get in with a knife or money. If they want to get in with money, they swallow the money, and when they get to prison they take a physic and get it out that way.

I think the best way to kill a man is just have a cool head. Use your head and have a little patience, and wait till you get him in the right spot. When he is in the right spot, you know what you have to do, and you can take him and kill him and get away.

My opinion of getting a leader is to walk right up and kill him, because you're not going to have any other chance in killing him. He has too many around him, and he is too careful.

I was once offered $20,000 off a man for to kill his wife. His wife was going for every Tom, Dick and Harry, and she was double-crossing him. I didn't want to do that because I knew he would get a pickup, and not knowing how he would stand with the cops. The best way I know to do such a thing would be to drive past with a car, pick her up, and be nice with her. Get her to a cabaret, let her gain your confidence. Try to induce her into an apartment. If lucky in doing so, such women know what's the consequence. You do not have to rape them.

Be nice to her and then tell her you are going to take her on a vacation. Take her to the mountains, the two of you together. Get yourself a room in a hotel, and every day go out to some part of the woods and dig yourself a big, big ditch. Then every day dig and dig until you know it is deep enough—about six feet—and take her and tell her you will take her for a walk through the woods, and when you reach this spot, take her and hit her on the head and knock her on the head and kick her into the hole, which is known as a grave, and throw dirt on her and bury her alive.

Before the murder, have her write a letter to her folks that she is running away, that she can't stand her husband and is going to run away. Naturally, her people get that letter and they know her circumstances. They are going to figure she did run away by not seeing her for a few days and by not hearing from her by mail. Time progresses along and they don't hear from her, figuring she must be in some city or country doing pretty good; but in the meantime she is dead, and nobody knows about it, and that is one way to get rid of a person.

I knew of a case where a fellow went to visit another fellow in Sing Sing Prison. His enemies knew he went to that prison on that day, and on his departure from the prison they knew he was going to get off the train at Yonkers, and then taxicab it down to some part of the city which is unknown. But while he got off the train at Yonkers, he got met by his foes and stuck up, and put into a car and drove out to the woods to some dead locality in Yonkers and killed and let lay in the grass.

Another thing, to kill a man you got to know how to shoot him. If you know a fellow is out to kill you, sometimes on the spur of the moment you may see him and open up on him and give it to him, when if you are a good head you will use your head and wait, because what is known as patience is a virtue and always keep a cool head. I know for myself, because I was looking to kill two people and they got smart to my idea, because one day I trusted a party and he went back and told. I always knew in my heart that that party was a rat, but I had a little confidence in him at that time, because you got to have confidence in somebody. He went and told them people and these people, on one night when I was looking for a gun, said to a friend of mine that had a car, they said: "Where's so and so, I'll give him a gun." While I was walking on the street a car drew up and they hollered my name. I came over, knowing that the driver of the car was a good, personal friend of mine. If not, I would never have walked over. When I walked over, one of the fellows in the car, which I didn't talk to, stepped out and says: "Hello, so and so, you want a gun?" I said: "Yes," and he shot me four times. That was the fellow I was out after. I figured he was looking to make up with me or something.

He shot me four times and he made to throw the gun into the car, but it fell into the mudgutter of the street. I walked away until stuck up by a cop. I said: "What are you putting up that thing to me, ain't I shot enough?" He said: "Who's doing all the shooting around here?" I said: "I don't know." They brought me to the hospital and said: "Who shot you?" I said: "I don't know, what's it your business who shot me?" because I hate a cop's face. The fellow is still walking the streets today, and I am alive. We are good friends today.

The day came for me to square up as to my shooting. I was looking for him and he was looking for me, but we never met. I used to go into cabarets, and friends of mine had to close up their places, knowing I would shoot him. Knowing I was hurt, I wanted to get even, and wouldn't let up until I would get even. One day a

very good friend of ours—a good friend of mine and a good friend
to him—says: "Listen, I want you to square this thing up." I said:
"Listen, I am shot, and the only time I'll square up is when I out
someone." He said: "What's the use of fighting, he didn't mean it.
He got steamed up to do it." So finally, I said O.K.

I came down myself without any gun, and walked into a place
where I knew there were three punks that I didn't have any use
for, and we started talking. I said what was on my chest and he
said what was on his chest, and we both spoke it out. I wanted to
know what I got shot for, and he told me—on account of this
steaming that I was looking to kill him. But I was looking for the
other two, to kill them, because they were no good and I didn't
like them. A friend of mine went to the can and I used to send him
money, and they wouldn't send him a nickel. I knew he was in jail
through them. I used to walk over to them and say: "Ain't you
going to send up so and so some money?" They would say: "We're
broke," and in the meantime they would tell me they lost three or
four thousand in a crap game. They said they were taking care of
him, but I knew they weren't.

So I was looking for them. So would anyone, if you are a
friend of mine and you are doing a bit for someone else. I know
he is making money and spending it—why can't he send you
something to live on, to buy cigarettes and food, which you can
buy in the commissary. A guy like that is no good.

I am meeting this friend of mine about a month later, and he
told me the story. I said: "Didn't I always tell you that he is a rat
and no good?" My words turned out to be right. And I said: "If you
are ever looking to kill him, let me kill him."

I was at a theatre uptown one afternoon and I seen the same
party that I never had any use for, although I didn't want to be
turned to be a double-crosser in killing him, as I promised I would
never hurt anybody in regard to that case. My words came true
that both of them were rats. One afternoon in the theatre uptown
I happened to be in the smoking room, and I happened to see the
same party come up with two detectives. Happened to hear them
holler out his name and ask: "What seats have you got?" He said:
"The best seats in the house." I recognized his voice and jumped
into a phone booth in the theatre and rung up his friends, and

notified them that so and so was up with cops. They said: "Are you sure?" They figured maybe I am looking to steam them up on him. I said: "Come up and I will let you use my ticket." I didn't trust him and trust the cops who was with him, because they were known as money cops. His supposed-to-be friends came up, and I gave them my ticket, and they went in and seen for themselves.

This is a Friday afternoon. On Sunday afternoon a car drew up to his house about four p. m., inviting him out to a party. He got dressed, his wife was very happy, he had a little kid, and he went into said car, on their way out to Long Island. He was asked questions on the way out. They didn't have him in the right position. If I was in the said car I would have him in the back, and not in the front. He was sitting at the right of the chauffeur, in the front. When they started firing questions at him as to his ratting, he got smarted up and opened the door without them knowing it. Then he jumped. In the meantime they fired four shots which hit him, three in the head and one in the back. He was lucky enough to come to in the hospital. He squealed as to who shot him in the car. He wound up in the can for being a rat with the cops. He got framed up, and got two and a half years.

That's a good way of killing a man—take him out on a supposed-to-be party and pump him full of lead, and let him lay in the bushes. Nobody knows the thing of it, providing you keep your mouth shut.

I know an enemy is in a cabaret. I would scheme out to have a cab or car waiting, to have a friend steal a cab and place it in front of a cabaret and stay there, and when so and so comes out of that cabaret, let him step in the cab. Take him out of the cab, chase the girl and knock her out on a side street, not letting her see our faces by putting a handkerchief in front of our faces. Then do with him as we want.

Another good way in getting rid of a guy is to keep in his confidence, treat him right, let him gain your confidence, carry around a little poison, and if he ever goes into a toilet, slip it into his food and kill him that way.

Another good way in killing a man with a gun is this. You don't like somebody. You know he is looking to get you. The next move is to use your head, as you naturally can tell when a person don't like you. I know if I don't like anybody I wouldn't walk on the same side of the street with him. I can't see into that smearing up business, because when they are smearing up with you, they are looking to kill you. The first thing you know, you might be on a spot in a cabaret or such a place, and walk into the lavatory and be stuck up with guns, which you know they have a silencer. And if there is a porter in the toilet, they stick him up and tie him up, and give it to you with a silencer and let you lay. Nobody gets caught for said crime unless a man opens up, and I know a dying man's confession is no good.

Another good way to kill a fellow is to wine him and dine him, show him that you are his friend, and when you get him set up in such a position as to take him or kill him, you give it to him and let him lay.

Another way is to steam him through a girl, through a friend of yours. Notify him that there is a broad up on the roof, like in the summer time. You say: "Come up and we'll get straightened out." When you get the party up on the roof you kill him, and there's no girl there; but there is a friend of yours on the roof waiting for your coming, and he kills the said party.

Another way to kill a man would be to wait in his hallway and have him surprised. Every person you hear walking up, you walk down. If it is not him, walk out to the street. You re-enter the building and walk out again until the man comes that you want. When the man comes that you want, you kill him and screw out and run into the street.

The next best thing to do in killing a man is to leave a gun on his person, which is a good case, because the Police Department of the City of New York says: "What the hell, that's another one gone," and the case is forgotten about. They don't interest themselves too much in the case where gangsters are killed.

Another way is to trail a man and see where his girl lives, if he has such. Have a car waiting, and when he meets said girl, if you want to take the risk—where the girl don't know said people that are killing him—you can kill him right there; but it is much better to use your head and wait until he leaves. You can do better then, and kill him without anybody knowing about it.

Here's another. One of my own cases. I was to a party one night. This fellow got a friend of mine killed for no good reason at all. After he got him killed, I asked: "Aren't you going to get even?" He said: "No, watch out, they're looking for you." The cops watched out and come up to me and says: "Danny, who killed so and so?" I said: "I don't know." I was surrounded by a bunch of cops, brought to the station, and questioned as to the killing of so and so. They gave me a subpoena to go to the District Attorney's office the following day, and gave me a smack in the mouth. I went to the District Attorney. Told him I don't know who killed so and so. The next day I said: "Are you going to get even, or not?" We were talking.

He was always known as a bulldozer in our neighborhood. People feared him. He would walk over and paste anybody.

He used to paste me on the eye, bust me on the chin once in a while. Naturally, one night I couldn't stand it any more, because he gave me a busted nose. I says to him: "I'm going to get even with you." That night I come down with a —— under my coat, figuring he was going to stop and hit me. He said to me: "I just socked somebody I didn't like." I said: "O.K." Nothing happened. The next night I was to a party. He was there. He said: "Sing a song, punk." I said: "I ain't no actor, I can't sing." He said: "Sing a song, you punk, you." I said: "I can't sing." He almost broke my arm. I said to myself: "I am going to get even with that bastard. I am going to kill him."

At that time I had a gambling joint running on the East Side. The next night he came into my place of business at three o'clock in the morning. I was in there with a Jewish fellow. He went up to him and busted him. I went over and said: "Why don't you use your head, why don't you go outside and fight instead of starting trouble in here?" I said that because I had my gun in the toilet, and would have got my gun and gone out in the street and killed him. He said: "Get the hell out of here," and give me a smack in the face. I was so mad and scared I didn't care what I did. I hit him in the mouth. I knocked him down. When he fell over, a gun fell out of his pocket. I picked it up and shot him three times, and he said: "Please, for my mother's sake." "Screw, kid," I said to my Jew friend. He screwed.

I figured I would bury him across the way in an empty lot. Later, I would hire out a horse and wagon, and take him out of the lot and throw him overboard, because he would be found in some part of the East River. My damn' luck—I happened to hail a cab driver to drive me to the lot. While I was upstairs getting the body, he ran away with a fifty dollar bill of mine which I gave him to drive me two blocks. So I carried it over there myself. I knew I had to work fast. So I proceeded in burying him in the empty lot.

Eventually I was in my place of business, and had the mattress I had put him on in the back room over my shoulder, which I took to the roof to burn up. As I was walking out of my side door I seen two blue uniforms. This cab driver came back with two cops. He said: "This's the house where the guy came out of." I ducked back. They knocked on the door, and said: "Open up!" I said: "Just a minute, my wife is dressing." I tiptoed through a side door to the store in front and got about twenty feet ahead of them. They followed and fired shots at me. I got away from them and ran up on a roof but couldn't get off the roof, so I ran down that house, down to a saloon I knew, and put a white apron on.

I told the saloonkeeper: "I got in plenty of trouble." He said: "All right," but told me to screw out. I went up to a friend of mine's house but he wasn't in. I went up on his roof. While there, two detectives came up. I was hiding behind a water-tank on the roof. The two detectives says: "There's nobody up here." I was about five feet away from where they were talking. They went down. I got a little scared, got from behind the tank, walked down the stairs, and while walking down four detectives were walking up. I walked right past them and ducked into this friend of mine's house and waited for him to come. When he come, and I told him what's what, he fainted. This guy is in the Death House now. He isn't going to die, though; he's goin' to get twenty to life.

When I told him what's what, he fainted and I got him up and he says: "Kid, you got to screw." I says: "O.K." Anyway, I walked all the ways through the East Side, over to Avenue C, then uptown. Got a Hudson Tube train to Jersey, and stayed in a house over there until the cops came to the house one day. I jumped out of the window and got back to New York. Got away to another friend of mine in the mountains. I stayed up in the country for three months—in Fallsburg, N. Y. I stayed at one of the swellest hotels in the mountains.

In the meantime my friends were taking care of my witnesses that were against me. They found out who they were. They would walk over to them and say: "If you ever say anything against so and so, your life isn't worth a nickel." They would walk over and tell them: "Listen, when so and so gets brought before you in the lineup, don't you say: 'That's him.' You say: 'This ain't the fellow I mean; the fellow I mean is another fellow and he had the same name as me.'" It took quite a while to get 'em all lined up. Then I came down to the city.

I seen detectives who didn't know who I was, but I knew who they were. I always held a cool head and had a smile for everybody. Naturally, one day the detectives that were assigned to my case came up to the house where I was, and I ducked out and beat it. The next thing I heard, the detectives seen me and passed me up. I stayed in the city for about two days and came back in the mountains again. I stayed there until notified to come in to give myself up.

I had a lawyer through my friends, but never seen him. I went to him and he said: "Did you kill so and so?" I got told to have confidence in this guy, he is O.K. I answered. He said: "You did not." I said: "All right, I didn't." He said: "Where were you on so and so a day?" I said: "Here." He said: "You were not. You were working." I said: "All right, I was working." Then I had to get a place to see where I was working, which I did through friends of mine.

I was supposed to be a truck driver. This man vouched that I worked on that night, and that I always worked from twelve midnight until eight a. m. in the morning, and the murder was committed around four o'clock in the morning. Naturally, that was a good alibi for me. The cops were to my house on the morning of the murder and I wasn't there. They told my mother to tell me to come to the station house. I said: "To hell with them, mom, if they want me, they know where to get me." That was my alibi at the trial. I swore blue Christ that I came in every morning at eight o'clock and slept from eight until four in the afternoon, unless I got up some afternoons to see a show, and then went back to sleep again until about eleven o'clock, as I worked in Jersey and didn't have to be there until twelve. The cops claimed they used to come to my house sometimes two or three times in a night, looking for me, never see me but seen my father and my brother. I fixed it up with them. They got five thousand dollars on that case.

Anyway, I was down in the heart of the city where I came from, and was supposed to be caught by detectives and was sent to a restaurant to wait. A couple of detectives happened to be in there that knew me. I had my face turned so they could see me. They bent down and turned my face around and said: "You're a nice kid." Anyway, they walked out and wanted to be seen with money. That night a murder was committed on the East Side, it was supposed by the late Dropper Kid. I was told by the detectives: "Hell, there ain't nothing in this today for us. You go home and be down tomorrow at the same time."

They were friends of mine, but I didn't know that. One of them broke his leg account of me—running after me; he always swore that if he would get me he would kill me and then take me in, on account of breaking his leg one day chasing me on the Williamsburg Bridge. I think I could have passed him up twenty times a day on the lower East Side, because I weighed 133 pounds at the time of the murder and I gained something like 22 pounds within the time I was away.

I came down the following morning. I was directed to go into a restaurant and they would come in and catch me, which they didn't. My friends came in and told me: "Listen, go over to the cigar store across the street and buy a cigar and stay there until they come over and catch you," which I did. Naturally, they came over and nabbed me. When they nabbed me, they took off my hat and said: "You are a nice-looking kid, but we want you for murder." I was directed to holler: "You are framing me!" so that a lot of people would hear me and I could have them for witnesses. I was then brought to the station house detective bureau, and the fellow said: "You didn't get fat sleeping on the East Side; where have you been?" I said: "I've been working every day and home every night." They said: "You are a liar." They didn't hit me, but I was instructed if I got a bat in the ear to take it and don't think they were turning on me. So they brought me down to the Homicide Bureau and said to keep my mouth shut.

I was brought before the Inspector, who said: "What's your name?" I told him. He said: "Ain't you got an alias?" I said: "No, sir, my name is what I am telling you." I said I knew a fellow by that name, but that I wasn't that fellow. He said: "Do you remember such and such a day?" I said: "Yes." He said: "Do you remember so and so?" I said: "Yes, he was a very dear friend of mine." He said: "Do you know what happened to him?" I said: "Only what I read in the papers and heard off friends." He said: "What did you hear?" I said: "The morning when he was found dead and buried in an empty lot." He said: "What were your friends talking about?" I said: "They were talking about arrangements for the funeral." I swore I gave money to buy flowers, which I did. I gave a few bucks to buy flowers. I had it in my heart to say I was even up to his house to visit him at his wake, but it didn't come to that. I didn't come out with that answer. When he asked about the killing I said: "I refuse to answer."

Then the detectives in the Homicide Bureau picked up chairs and held them a few inches over my head like they were going to beat me up, and I said to myself: "It is better to keep tight than to get burned in the chair," which I knew in my heart I would beat the case. He said: "What are you smoking cigarettes so frequently for, are you nervous?" I said: "No, I'm just a habitual smoker." They let me sit near an open window, figuring I would jump out and they could shoot at me. I was too smart for them. In the meantime detectives were coming in and saying: "Hello, so and so," which I wouldn't answer. I would only answer to my right name.

After you kill a man, go to a lawyer that can be trusted. Your lawyer schemes out. He tells you to walk in and give yourself up and refuse to answer any questions put to you. That's the way to beat the case. When you are brought before the cops and they ask you: "You are charged with killing so and so." "I never killed him," and you always have a perfect alibi where you were that night.

Make it up yourself. You can go and get yourself two tickets for a show. Give them to two friends of yours. Pick a bill that you seen. Just have a young lady take the stand that she accompanied you to the show at the time of the killing.

Naturally, to convict a man it takes four eyes and not two, unless it's a case of circumstantial evidence. Supposing a man is wanted for a crime of murder. The best thing to do would be to obtain yourself a good mouthpiece, which is known as a lawyer and, naturally, he has to work with your friends. He's got to work with your friends, and whoever you see the District Attorney calls down for a witness in the said case of murder. Your own friends try to pull a connection with them—go over and talk to them and bring them down to your lawyer. Then he gets a story out of them and he has them sign it—their own version of the murder. The said witness is told what he said.

Naturally, he don't want to show himself a rat, fearing that he would get hurt or killed, so he does as he is told. Sometimes they are given money for this, or if they are ignorant they do it for nothing. They sign that confession, which the lawyer keeps. He makes a duplicate and an original and he keeps them until the time for a trial, if the defendant goes to trial, which is presented before the Grand Jury and the Court.

After committing a murder, if anybody sees you, you always wait and have a connection to find out who is who in the case, which can be easily found out with a few bucks. I know of a case where a girl was a witness in a shooting of a leading politician in New York City. He was known to be a boozer and a gangster before being a politician. He was noted to be a hell of a nice fellow while sober, but while drunk he was a mean son of a bitch.

One day he sent for a certain party that was wanted by the police to come in to him and give himself up, which he did. He came in, and they happened to go to a cabaret in the Bronx. There was a couple of girls in the party. I guess he wanted to show he could be boss over the fellow. This fellow was nagging at him all night, and the fellow couldn't stand it. He said: "Lend us your gun." He did, and he turned around and killed him. After killing him he dropped the gun right near his side. When the homicide cops came they moved the gun twenty feet away from the dead body, which would make it look stronger against the party that killed him. That fellow got caught a couple of days later in an apartment—a Wop. He didn't open up, this Wop terming it was self-defense—that he pulled a gun and he pulled it out of his hand and killed him. He got discharged.

I remember on the East Side, one evening a fellow got shot three times—two in the back and one in the arm. An innocent bystander got killed, but the said fellow that did the shooting got away in a car. He got caught about an hour later and got arrested for the crime. The fellow that was shot didn't identify the same, but a cop that was interested in the case had a girl that was working in a theatre, that was an usher, and he asked her to take the stand against this here fellow and to swear against his life that he was the one that killed this fellow, and when she seen the shooting that she wasn't working that afternoon.

The cop told her to say that. The lawyer on the defense looked into the case, and seen that the only way out was to try to term her as a prostitute, which would show a more better reason and possibly a grievance between her and the fellow that was held for the charge. Here's how they schemed. They found this here broad was living with this cop. They turned around and sent a friend of theirs up to said girl's apartment, rang her bell, which she answered and came and opened the door. She said: "What do you wish, sir?" Anyway, he got inside, and when he left he handed her a ten dollar bill which was marked.

Naturally, they had their own detectives with them that would make the pinch, and some bull cries that she's a prostitute and that he seen this fellow in the bedroom with her. Naturally, to make her a prostitute, which would help him at the trial to prove that she was a prostitute. This broke down her testimony as to her saying she was an eye-witness to the said crime of murder, and where the lawyers on the defense brought out that she lived with the said copper—which the said fellow got discharged.

If you were a witness to a case I was interested in, I would get my friends to try to locate you and act nice to you and to try to get in connection with somebody that would know you, for us to get properly introduced, and take you out and wine you and dine you and show ourselves regular fellows with you. If money was the object, we would produce it and give it to you, providing the said man would get discharged, which would be put in reliable hands to a party that you know and I know, and on said dismissal of the case you would get it. If no dismissal, I would get it. I would take you down to the defendant's lawyer and have you say what we would want to say, and for you to sign, which is very useful in the case of a murder charge. We would believe in you, and if you turned we would know our next move.

If you weren't interested in money, then we would look to talk to you, and if you went down and made a holler, then we would know our next move, which would be to kill you to save our friend's life and his liberty. In a murder case you often start in by killing one, and you might kill a dozen. The papers come out with it: "Another gangster shot."

Take some case where a fellow is a material witness, is held for the House of Detention—a place where nobody can get to him, not even his own, immediate family. There is a bail set on such a person. The best move is to get him out on bail, so that you can talk to him, so that you can have him say what you would want to say. That person may see he has confidence in you, and you get him to change the testimony he gave the Grand Jury, to say he was beat up by the cops and tortured to testify against you—to give such testimony as he did before the Grand Jury.

Take him into your confidence and treat him or her nice. Give them an allowance of money, which maybe looks very big to them but which may be very small to you, and which maybe you wouldn't miss. You get them to say what you would want them to say, and take them down to the defense lawyer. He gets a statement from them as to their version at the time of the murder, which shows they were mistreated by the police—as to be hit and bulldozed into a confession through fear.

He is told that when you come to identify the said person—which is naturally held in the Tombs Prison in the City of New York—they hold what is called a lineup in the Tombs. They call out all the persons of your height and description. You are placed in a line at the said time of lineup, there is an Assistant

District Attorney, his stenographer, the detective assigned to the case, the warden of the prison and the keeper of the tier of the said prisoners. The witness is told to walk up and back the line and to see if he can point out his prisoner. He or she knows enough not to pick out the right person, and says: "He's not here."

That is sufficient for the warden of the said institution in which the witness is brought down. He or she don't pick out nobody. Naturally, if the prisoner is brought into Court of the City of New York, it is a good out as to why don't they pick the prisoner out on the lineup. As you know, murder is a tough case to be convicted of in the City of New York. The witness knows that you are in the lineup, and with fear in his heart he doesn't pick you out. He or she comes downstairs with the said District Attorney, stenographer, warden and detective, and is let out again until further questioning.

You are presented in Court, witnesses are brought before you, placed on the stand, which face you face to face. The Court orders such a witness to take a good look at the said prisoner to see if he is the man, which they turn you frontwards, sideways and backwards to see if they can identify you, and they say: "No, that ain't the man that I seen. The man was much taller or much smaller or much fatter." This point is a good out for the said man held for murder, because the said witness is either getting paid off with money, or threatened, as to his identifying the said prisoner.

You have to work in with somebody. Ninety-nine percent of the cops are O.K. as far as business is concerned. To tell you the truth, the most regular cops I ever met, that without a nickel, without good connections, was in Cleveland. They just treat you right. The out-of-town cop has more respect for a fellow that is connected a little than the copper over here. A cop in this city is too respected, he respects himself too much and other people respect him too much. You know there are some cops in New York that are made without political influence. If you talk to the out-of-town copper, he's got to listen to a politician.

To my opinion, a cop that don't take it, maybe you can go over his head and get out that way. I mean you can get to the Judge and have the minutes of the case changed around. When the complainant makes out the complaint, he don't see it any more until the Judge gets it. After that he never sees the complaint.

It's only the unfortunate who suffers. I mean, if a guy ain't got nobody behind him, and is what is known in the underworld as a tramp or a bum and nobody behind him, the cops look to get rid of him to make themselves a name. I won't say they frame him, but they look to make the evidence a little stronger in order to try to convict the man when he has tried to pull off a murder.

They won't never talk business with you, you have to get some other people to talk business with them, that they have confidence in.

Thousands of dollars is paid out that way, on one case. Take a case of murder, a cop generally gets plenty of thousands for changing his testimony or keeping quiet. There is always two coppers assigned to a case. One watches the other, and what one gets they both split.

If they know you are making money, they come over and give you a phony pickup. Them phony pickups are worse than a real pinch, because the man don't know what the hell way to move. The only best move, he says to himself, these cops are out for dough, and they got to get it. And if they don't get it, they have a rapper there to identify you.

The only way is to use your head—is to have yourself a good alibi fixed as to where you were at the time of the shooting. As far as the punks squealing—you weren't there. Your word is as good as their word. Another thing, you would have the money to supply for your word. You have the connections to beat the case.

Chapter 16
WHY I WON'T WORK

Why should I work? Look what I have gone through. I went through more than any guy living, as far as the underworld is concerned. I was close to death on several occasions. But I am still here.

I was never out for glory, and was always out for the buck. I made all of my money through gambling and bootlegging; and so far as stealing, it cost me more than I ever made. You'll get away with it today and you may get away with it tomorrow, but when you get caught, you'll pay for three times—not the two times that you got away. Still and all, when I came out of Elmira, I was supposed to do two years parole, and they see that you work every day. With me, I reported one year and got out of the rest of it.

Crime does not pay because the best you wind up is behind the eight ball. The cops are going to look to pin things on you. No matter whether you do anything or not, you will wind up in the can anyway, if you have no dough. They know that you can't make a good egg out of a rotten egg. But I'll say that if you got it in you to be bad, you will be bad, and the only way to be good is through your own self. If you don't listen to your own father or mother, it is a sure thing you won't listen to them. As they say, it pays to learn. How does a racket guy give pay? He either pays with his life or pays by going to prison.

Who do you think does the business with your unions? You think the worker, when he gets hit in the strike. It's only a lousy punk hits him. It ain't the smart guy. That punk is maybe getting fifteen bucks a day for going and doing that kind of work; and then there's a go-between, that's in with the union, that's getting big dough for that. And the guy that's the go-between is considered the big guy in the union, and the punk they don't want to know. The union guys don't care who does the job, they don't care as long as it's done, but big dough is given up for that. In some cases it's a guy with a good head carries them punks around—to carry a gun for him. You don't have to pay them the same as a good fellow. They're satisfied if you let them in your company.

Between you and I, I was a fellow that the only ones I would consider my friends are fellows that I know since I am a kid. A new face, new fancy, I never went for. Although sometimes strangers will help you out more than your own best friends, which is known throughout the West. Take a fellow that is pinched for a robbery or murder, and if he don't open up, he will have people step to the front for him and he won't even know. I myself would take care of the fellow that was still in. I would stick to him like a brother.

The fellows that don't, they're no good. They could give money to a friend of his, or someone else, to send him up a bunch of foodstuffs or so. Maybe the fellow might not take it, fearing poison. Then make a connection to give the money to his wife, if he is married, or to his girl, and not let him know where it came from.

One thing I can truthfully say, I hate a rat in my heart, and have said so plenty of times, and I wouldn't open up on said person and they wouldn't open up on me. Why should I? I'll take care of him myself. If I get killed, that's my hard luck.

That's in my heart, I wouldn't squeal on nobody. I wouldn't care if I got killed in this apartment. If I was living just enough to talk, and was asked: "Yes or no?" I would say: "No." They are a bunch of son of a bitches that would squeal. Those people that want to talk should go to work. They wouldn't get shot and wouldn't have to squeal. Now I don't trust nobody—very few of them. I could know you for years and years and never tell you what I do.

A fellow that's in this racket, he ain't outspoken, but I'm a type that's outspoken, and I tell a guy to his face. I ain't the type that looks for trouble, and if trouble comes my way, I know I will kill the bastard with his face down in the grave.

One thing I can say—I hate a cheap, cheap thief. I know for myself if people come to me and say: "Listen, I got so and so a trick," and I know in my heart that I am hard up and can't get a thousand dollars for my end, I don't go, but I'm always looking for better. I'm looking for that buck.

Sometimes the rap ain't so bad. I remember a case of a guy in a racket with those old stamps. He had a process of erasing the cancellation. He made a million dollars. The fellow got pinched for it and is in Atlanta now. I think he got five years. You get a third time off for good behavior, and if you got dough you can live in them places better than you can out here. Another case: I seen a guy that laid up there in Sing Sing, and had it better than some people living outside. He had his own little cottage on the hill, and had his women come to see him. He had his own cooks.

I hate a guy that works on a sure thing. He won't take a chance, although I give any guy credit that can stay out of the can. I give him all the credit in the world. I mean a guy who will wait, and wait and wait. He won't work and he won't steal. He's waiting for God to drop him down a package. If you declare him in on something, he knows in his heart he isn't going to get a pinch. That's what I mean by a sure thing.

There are some guys that if you pat them on the back, would kill a guy for you. You can get the biggest man in the country killed if you treated them good. I never look to mingle with that kind, because I never had no use for a punk like that. I believe if a guy kills a guy, he should have a reason for it. To kill a guy just to make a good fellow of yourself in some other people's eyes is no good, because in their heart they are only thinking you a punk for doing it. On the opposite side, he thinks he did them the greatest favor for putting a guy out of the way.

Any guy with sense who comes to you and says: "Listen, I'll kill that guy for you," and he goes and kills him, you got to watch him, because he might kill you, too. You treat them good, show them good, and then show them a little bad, and they will turn on you like a dog. You show them bad and then show them good, they'll think you are the best guy in the world.

I did want to go straight at one time. I got myself a job in the newspaper line. I gave up the job because cops came around and were bothering me. They made me quit. I happened to be working on the circulation end of a newspaper—count the bundles, etc. I got myself a job down there and was making $105 a week. In a newspaper racket, they are known to pay big money for their help. It calls for a guy to get that salary, and they paid me that salary. They pay because they know that I would not work for less. They want me especially because they have faith in me.

I used to guard a circulation manager, other managers, and a superintendent of delivery. I acted as sort of a bodyguard for them. I was looking to see that they didn't get hurt. They would look to bounce guys, and would have a lot of trouble, strikes, etc. There was a circulation manager in there, and he was noted as an efficiency expert, and he was bouncing men, and this and that, and in that racket guys fight for that job—you must fight.

A fellow got himself a job as a superintendent, and that circulation manager wanted him because he knew that he was a good man. He knows who is a good man. He is responsible for getting complete distribution of the papers. I was known to be the Assistant Superintendent to him. I worked there, and got a good break when I stayed there a half-hour a night. There is a lot of jealousy. A fight started, and I nearly got poisoned. They were looking to kill me. There was another guy who was an assistant foreman. He had an argument with an assistant circulation manager. This guy didn't stand for it, and called down the cops. Just before that, a guy got a cut on the face.

The cops came around and said: "Who cut so and so?" They said: "We heard you cut him." I said: "I'll kill that guy if he comes near this plant. What is he looking to make a holler for?" The night before, he fired two shots at me and I didn't run for the cops. That caused a lot of trouble. They overlooked it. But there was a fight going on between the circulation manager of the *New York* —— and the President of the Union. This circulation manager of the *New York* —— said to me: "Why don't you work for me, and I'll give you so much?" But I liked the other side better. I was getting more money. I knew I had an easy thing here, and it was a good job.

The cops came down. This guy was a big shot. It was through him that I lost the job. The paper didn't fire me or tell me; but they sent down cops, and they came down either five or six different times. One night they laid for me by my house in the summer time, when I was coming home about four o'clock in the morning on a Saturday. I happened to just get out of a cab. I knew they were looking for me at the newspaper plant. They happened to catch me. "Here he is—here is our meat." They banged me and I got up, and they dropped me again. They said: "Throw him into a car." One questioned me. What good was his questioning, and what good was my answering? They told me I was a God damn' liar. I would get hit again. He said: "Listen, how did you get a union card?" I worked in this racket all the time. I told them I got $48 or $50 a week, as I was only on the books for that amount in the paper. He said to me: "You are a liar." I said: "Why should I argue with you fellows—go down and look at the books. I never look to bulldoze any of the drivers." I would see that they got back to work tomorrow if they got bounced.

I always got taken in the end from those fellows. They would run away with the collections. That was my job to get those guys. He said to me: "Listen, you are always carrying a gun." I said: "If I want to carry a gun, I can go out and make money and carry a gun." He said: "If I ever catch you with a gun I will put it down your throat." I said: "I won't let any lousy cop get me. I'll shoot it out with him."

I went to a party to get myself straightened out with the detective, so that I would not be bothered any more. I could have started a lot of trouble for them, although I may not have got the best of it. A lot of people were telling me, like the superintendent of the newspaper: "Go down to Police Headquarters and make a holler. I want you to work with me, you are working straight." I knew the newspaper racket. I knew it very, very good. I would have been up on top and I would not have had to carry a gun and get shot. Why should I make myself 15,000 enemies as far as the Police Department is concerned, because they would say: "That God damn' rat, he don't like to get hit." They would send me to jail. It was never in me to squeal on the cops.

I had it in my heart not to let them get away with it. I said I never got a deal like that. I said I would never work again. Then and there I got so God damn' disgusted I said I would be worse now than I was ever in my life. I got pinched.

They said: "What do you do for a living?" I said: "I gamble." The judges said: "You are a gambler?" and I said: "Yes, I would not work for Jesus Christ. Why should I work after all that I went through? I won't get nothing working any more. I went through the whole thing."

I was told to go in to work, that everything was straightened out. I was working ten minutes when the cops hit me on the body with bundles of newspapers and so on. They told me I was getting money on false pretenses, and didn't want me to work. They pestered me so much. I was lucky I could walk Broadway without being stopped by them and getting busted. What could I do if they did such a thing? I would have to take it and keep my mouth shut. If I do get hit now, I know that I have done something to get hit, and I'll take it.

Crime does not pay because you never wind up with anything. The best is, you are going to get hurt some way, you will go to the can, and no matter how good you are to some people, you are a punk to another, and probably that guy will look for revenge to get you out of the way, so that he can make that buck. They are a bunch that are jealous, and you don't know who to trust. You wind up only in the can, killing someone—or the chair.

Crime does not pay. There are your prisons. They are over flooded now. If crime paid, they would not be there. You don't get hurt through cops or courts, you get hurt through other people.

When you get that pinch, you must obtain the money, you must have good friends to get the money. Crime does not pay, because if you make it you are going to throw it away anyway. Ninety-nine percent of them are gamblers, and you wind up losing your money. You wind up getting killed or electrocuted. You throw it away in cabarets, you are a habitual drunkard, and you turn out to be a pipey; and it does not pay.

I am not smart enough to go into politics, though also I have political influence. I never told anybody in my life that I have a cousin, a leading politician. I always deny that he is my cousin, and I never told anybody. I didn't want to let my own people know that I was pinched. I have made money, but I didn't get anything out of life. There are no two guys living that saw what I have seen, and still I wound up with nothing in the end anyway. I always spend my money to go to other people that were connected in politics, but never to that politician;—I always deny that he is my cousin. I don't bother with him. If you should go to him and say: "Kid, I want to go straight," he won't believe me, and I would not work unless I could make a dollar.

In my opinion, on account of my misfortune as to getting arrested so many times, crime does not pay, as I think that the guy that is working for $50 a week is better off than his making for himself $10,000 in a year. He is going to throw it away like a salary. If he worked for the dollar, he would know the meaning of a dollar.

I give the guy credit that is in business. You don't get nothing working, unless you are getting a big salary. I have been used to too much money. I get a lot of money, but I give back twice as much to the cops.

I made my money through gambling. From now on, I intend to gamble. I'll gamble until the day I die. From now on my motto is: Plenty of women, plenty of cabarets, and plenty of gambling, with booze on the side.

THE END

New and Forthcoming Titles
From Staccato Crime

Made in the USA
Monee, IL
31 July 2023